newrooms

newrooms

A practical home makeover guide

Sally and Stewart Walton

p

This is a Parragon Publishing Book

This edition published in 2003

Parragon Publishing

Queen Street House

4 Queen Street

Bath BA1 1HE, UK

Created and produced for Parragon by The Bridgewater Book Company Ltd.

Creative Director Stephen Knowlden

Art Director Michael Whitehead

Editorial Director Fiona Biggs

Project Editor Sarah Bragginton

Designer Alistair Plumb

Photography Alistair Hughes

Picture Research Lynda Marshall

Illustrations Stewart Walton

ISBN: 0-75256-483-8

Printed in China

Contents

Introduction

A 1950s breakfast bar is just one of the many inexpensive projects you can do by following the step-by-step instructions in this book.

You don't need to go out and buy new furniture to give a room a new look. A new throw like this one on an elderly sofa can introduce strong color contrasts and a more relaxed style, as well as covering marks on old upholstery.

In the past, decorating was seen as a necessary chore, but these days it has become one of the most popular leisure activities. The aim of this book is to make decorating your home simple, inexpensive, and more fun than ever before. We live in the age of the make-over, and there has never been more choice available to the home decorator than there is now. There are more materials, books, television programs, and magazines about decorating and interior design that there have ever been

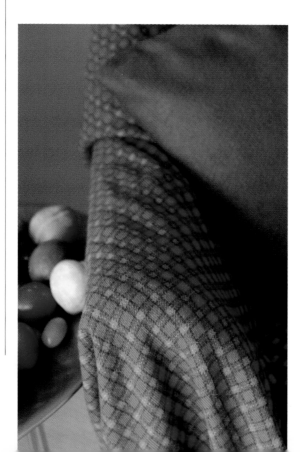

before, and the only downside is that there is often too much choice when it comes to deciding what you want! It is easy to make a decision about a color if there are only ten to choose from, but if you are faced with 200 subtle variations of blue, it's enough to confuse even the most experienced decorator.

The best way to stay sane and enjoy the decorating process is to have a clear idea of what you want and what you are going to do before you hit the stores. This means taking time to decide on color, style, and content by watching the television programs, looking in magazines and stores, then finding out how to get the look you're after by following the well-designed and inspirational step-by-step projects in this book.

New Rooms takes you through the entire home, offering a choice of traditional or contemporary ideas for each room. Many of the ideas will easily translate into other decorative styles, and can be adapted for use in other parts of the house. As many techniques are covered as possible; for example, the various flooring options that are available have been allocated to certain rooms, but the process of painting a wooden floor will be the same, whether done in a kitchen or a bathroom. You may well find that the ideal storage solution for your kitchen is one that is suggested in the nursery section, so be sure to have a look at all the projects before making up your mind.

The step-by-steps have been kept as clear and concise as possible—it is usually the case that too many instructions are as confusing as too few. As most decorating products come complete with their own set of instructions, these have been taken as read in many cases, and the step-by-steps just show how to put the actual idea into practice. The most vital product and tool instructions and advice to follow are those that relate to your safety. The statistics for decorating accidents in the home show that many

could have been avoided if only the safety advice had been followed.

So, if you plan to do up a whole house, decorate a room from scratch, or just make stylish improvements, we hope this book gives you with all the inspiration and information that you need.

Practical storage solutions like this disguised drawer on casters can be adapted for different rooms in the house, from the office to children's bedrooms.

Kitchens

The kitchen is often regarded as the heart of the home. It is the room where meals are prepared and is often a place to eat, gather, and socialize, so function plays a large part in the style. This section shows you how to transform your kitchen into three different styles: Country, Contemporary, and 1950s. Every kitchen can achieve these styles, whatever its size or shape, but an additional section shows you how to make the most of a galley kitchen. The three step-by-step projects will start you off, and a few accessories and a fresh coat of paint will do the rest. Have fun!

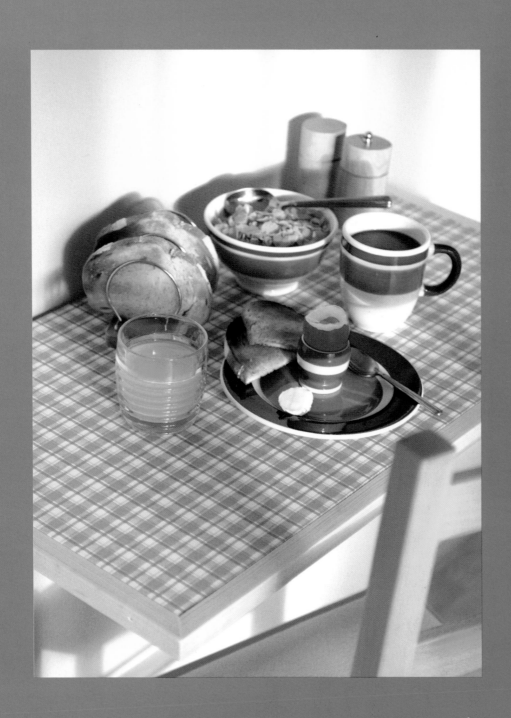

Country kitchen

For most of us, country living is a bit of a daydream, and if there is one aspect we would like more than anything it is the traditional country kitchen. The idea of sitting at a large, scrubbed, pine table, with the smell of baking and jars of home-made pickles and jam on the shelves, is very appealing, especially when your own kitchen has fitted melamine with all the charm of a school canteen! Don't despair, though; that country kitchen of your dreams may not be possible, but there is a lot that can be done to inject any kitchen with all the key ingredients.

Begin by listing the top 10 features that say "country" to you, loud and clear. They might go something like this…

1 Gingham
2 Baskets
3 Pine table and chairs
4 Old-fashioned sink with brass faucets
5 Wooden dish drainer
6 Curtains instead of blinds
7 Open shelves or a dresser
8 Solid fuel cooker
9 Busy walls with a display of plates
10 Stone-tiled floor

Realistically, your existing kitchen may be too small for a table and chairs, the floor may not be strong enough to support a solid fuel cooker, and you may have to make do with your stainless steel sink and the vinyl floor, but this doesn't mean that you can't go country in other ways. There are loads of things you can do to make a practical, modern kitchen feel more homely.

Natural colors

Start with the color, and if it is bright, white, and shiny it can be mellowed with a soft yellow wash, while if it is too boring and beige it can be spiced up with rusty red. Country colors are never harsh, and tend to echo nature and the countryside. Stencilled patterns make a very good background to the busy look that is so typically country. And more is definitely better when it comes to hanging pictures, plates, and kitchen utensils on the walls.

Soft lighting

Lighting can also make a real difference. You certainly need to see what you're doing and there is no denying that spotlights are useful, but they are also real atmosphere killers. A simple wrought-iron candelabra or a frosted-glass shade hung low over the table will create a more relaxed feeling, especially when fitted with a dimmer switch to vary the brilliance.

On display

A key aspect of the country look is having lots on show. You may not own a large dresser loaded with crockery, but a couple of wide plank shelves above a base unit can soon be dressed up to look like one. Simply paint the wall, shelves, and cupboard below the same color, add rows of cup hooks below the shelves and brass drawer handles, and then make a display of your kitchen crockery.

You can buy rolls of self-adhesive vinyl in gingham checks, using it to line drawers and shelves. Invest in a good quality, checked PVC

A pine table and chairs, a solid fuel cooker, and open shelves of crockery are features of a typical country kitchen, but there are other ways you can adopt the country style and give your kitchen a more homely feel.

tablecloth, and look around for odd wooden chairs in junk stores, and then paint them all the same color to make a nonmatching set.

Distressed paintwork

Distressed paintwork is still one of the key features in the country style because it gives the impression of having both a family history and a relaxed attitude. Fake it by applying contrasting colored paint in two coats, and sanding away the top coat in places to simulate wear and tear. Use flat paint and finish it off with a topcoat of beeswax polish, which looks and smells heavenly.

Country kitchens should also feel cosy in the evenings, so ditch the blinds and choose curtains instead. Shaker-style patterned fabrics featuring ticking stripes, tiny checks, or plaid patterns will all look good in the kitchen, and if you have a sewing machine, a simple plain border and some hand-stitched button detailing will add a contemporary touch. Some matching curtain ties in the same fabric will complete the look.

THE PROJECTS

The three projects on the following pages will help you achieve a country-style background in your own kitchen. A few carefully selected accessories, a fresh coat of paint, and some warm, relaxed lighting will do the rest.

More is better than less in a country-style kitchen, so have as much as possible on display. Cover wall space with shelves of crockery, cups on hooks, and small wooden cupboards, and replace modern drawer handles with brass versions.

YOU WILL NEED:

• ³/₈-IN. MDF

• FINE-GRADE
  SANDPAPER

• FACE MASK

• JIGSAW

• ⁵/₆-IN. DRILL BIT

• ALL-SURFACE PRIMER

• PAINT (SEMIGLOSS OR
  EGGSHELL FINISH)

• ENAMEL ROLLER AND
  SMALL ROLLER TRAY

• ¹/₂-IN. CHICKEN WIRE
  (OR NEAREST GAUGE
  TO THIS)

• WIRE CUTTERS

• SMALL HAMMER

• STAPLE GUN

PROJECT ONE

Replacing existing doors with chicken wire, framed in MDF

This project is suitable for wall-mounted kitchen or base units. If you like the look you could use it throughout the kitchen, but remember that you can see through chicken wire and not everything in a cupboard makes a good display.

Begin by emptying the cupboard and unscrewing the door. Kitchen cupboard hinges tend to leave large holes that will need filling if you are changing the style. Clean the inside of the cupboard with a grease-cutting detergent and paint it a country color—pale moss green or slate blue, for instance. Melamine will need to be primed first, ideally with an all-surface primer. If you are lining the shelves, do it at this stage before the door is replaced.

Replacing existing cupboard doors with chicken wire suits the country-kitchen look because it puts more of your kitchen on show. It's a good idea to plan the contents of the cupboards before you put them on display.

HOW TO DO IT

STEP 1 Place your outgoing door on top of the MDF. Use it as as a template, drawing the outline onto the MDF. Clamp the MDF on a workbench and wear the mask as you cut it to size, and sand the edges lightly.

STEP 2 Draw the cut-out shape onto the MDF. Drill a hole in one corner of the shape, using an 5/16-in. drill bit.

STEP 3 Clamp the MDF to the workbench and jigsaw out the inside shape. Keep the jigsaw's foot in touch with the surface of the MDF, and move with the saw.

STEP 4 Use sandpaper to smooth the edge on the inside and outside. Always wear a mask when sanding MDF to prevent you breathing in the fine particles which contain chemicals best avoided!

STEP 5 Give the door two coats of primer, following the drying times as directed on the can. Use a foam roller to apply the paint because it will give a better finish than a brush, and painting takes half the time. Apply the top coat in the same way.

STEP 6 Cut the chicken wire to the size of the cut-out shape, allowing an extra 1 in. all around the edge. Turn over a seam of 3/8 in. and flatten it with a hammer. Lay the MDF face down with the chicken wire in position at the back. Staple the panel at the four cardinal points first, then add more staples in between until it is perfectly secure. Re-hang the door.

TIP
• Chicken wire, even with a folded seam, has sharp, pointed edges. So long as the shelves in the cupboard are set back from the door, it is a good idea to cover up these edges with a simple wooden molding.
• Measure the lengths required, then miter the corners and use brads to secure them.

14

PROJECT TWO

Removing cupboard doors and adding willow baskets

Any base unit or kitchen cupboard can be given a real country look by removing the doors, and using willow baskets on the shelves as pull-out drawers. In fact, it may require a leap of the imagination to convert a standard beige melamine cupboard into something beautiful, but it can be done! All you need do is take off the doors, fill the holes, and pop in the baskets, but a few trimmings will make all the difference.

A melamine cupboard can be painted after suitable priming, and the facing edges of the cupboard can be covered with a wooden molding. They come in a range of styles, from twisted rope and oak leaves to simple half-moon and square edge. The inside of the cupboard will look good painted in a contrasting color to the outside, and there is also the option of adding a curtain on a simple net wire. Checked gingham or even linen tea towel curtains look a million times better than old melamine, and they can be tied back to reveal the baskets inside.

Willow baskets as sliding, pull-out shelves transform standard melamine cupboards. Paint the insides and outsides of the cupboard first, and add wooden molding to the facing edges.

HOW TO DO IT

STEP 1 Unscrew the existing doors and remove the fittings. Fill the holes with wood filler so that the filler stands slightly proud of the surface. Once it has dried, sand the filler level.

STEP 2 Measure the frame, then cut the molding to fit, mitering the corners. Apply contact adhesive to the frame.

STEP 3 Stick the molding down and then add a few pins along each length. Tap the pinheads into the molding with a center punch, fill the holes, and sand smooth.

STEP 4 Prime the cupboard and then paint it inside and out. If you are using two different colors, paint the inside of the cupboard first, and allow it to dry before painting the area where the colors meet.

BASKET HANDLE IDEAS
You can use any of the following...
• Cardboard parcel labels tied on with string
• Checked ribbons
• Stitched tubes of fabric
• Threaded beads or buttons on twists of wire
• Rope loops
• Buckled leather straps

STEP 5 Buy willow baskets to fill the space across the width, leaving just enough room for them to slide easily in and out. Many baskets have handles attached, but if not there are plenty of ways to make your own.

PROJECT THREE

Tiling a worktop

One thing you won't find in a perfect country kitchen is a vinyl laminated worktop. Wood or tiles are the look to go for, but the wood has to be well seasoned and solid, which is expensive. Tiles are the better option, and laying them on a flat surface is not only easy but fun. They will give you the country look for next to nothing and have maximum makeover power. The worktop is edged with a "hockey-stick" molding that has a flat edge and a rounded top resting on top of the tile, giving a very neat, professional finish.

Choose traditional-style, plain, deep greens or blues, or cream for the dairy look. Stone tiles are another option, but grease will mark them, so keep them away from the cooking area. A cheap and cheerful idea is to buy a range of different-color tiles that are all the same size. End-of-line tiles are often sold off cheaply and can be laid to look like a patchwork quilt pattern. Most importantly, measure the area that needs tiling carefully and buy the correct number of tiles to fit the space.

Tiles are one of the easiest and cheapest ways of giving your worktops a country-kitchen makeover. Edge them with a "hockey-stick" molding to give a neat, professional finish.

HOW TO DO IT

STEP 1 Have a trial run by laying out the tiles to get an idea of their spacing. Ideally you will have bought tiles that fit snugly to the edges of the worktop. If you do need to do any cutting, borrow a good tile cutter because it will make the job so much easier.

STEP 2 Spread ceramic tile adhesive over the surface to an even depth of about ⅜-in. Shape the surface of the adhesive into ridges with a spreading tool.

STEP 3 Press the tiles into the bed of the adhesive, beginning at the front corner, working along the front, and then filling in the rows behind. Aim to leave an equal gap between the tiles. Wipe off any adhesive that squeezes out while it is still wet, and then leave to set.

STEP 6 Apply contact adhesive to the front edge of the worktop. Rest the top of the molding on the tiles, and flatten it down onto the adhesive at the front. Fit two sides the same way, then tap in a few brads to help secure them, and punch their heads below the surface with a center punch. Fill the small holes, and then paint or varnish the molding.

STEP 4 Apply a generous amount of the grouting mixture, working it into the gaps between the tiles. Wipe off most of the excess with a damp sponge, and leave to set. Wipe again when it is semi-dry.

STEP 5 Measure the lengths of molding you need, and cut the adjoining pieces to a 45° angle with a miter saw. Only the front corners need mitering if the worktop is to stand against the wall.

Contemporary kitchen
The contemporary kitchen is a fusion between professional catering style and the comforts of home. This is the antidote to clutter and the minimalist's idea of heaven. It may seem impossible to maintain this chic, modern look, keeping worktops free of clutter, but with well-planned storage space and a little daily discipline, it can be easier than you think to achieve the contemporary style.

The best tables in a contemporary kitchen are simple foldaways or small, round, café-style versions, which do not interfere with the clean lines.

At its most extreme, the look is cold and industrial with steel, concrete, glass, and large, no-frills appliances that mimic a restaurant kitchen. The irony is that it is a style favored by wealthy, urban loft-dwellers who eat out most of the time! However, in the same way that haute couture inspires mainstream fashion, the extreme version of industrial chic is the inspiration for a more practical, comfortable, and achievable home style. The top 10 elements to go for are…

Stainless steel appliances
They echo the catering style but are scaled down to a more realistic size, while worktops are granite or marble, or resin compounds that look the part but are not as heavy or expensive as the real thing. Accessorize with stainless steel handles, utensils, light fittings, and sink units. Small details like stainless steel sockets and shelf supports will also make a big impact.

Stainless steel appliances and granite or marble worktops bring the professional catering style into the home. Stainless steel handles, utensils, light fittings, and sink units add to the impact.

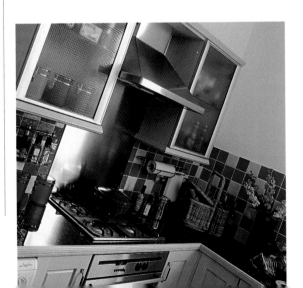

Pale wooden units
Plain, pale wood like beech or ash provides a perfect complement to steel, and this is where the homely look breaks ranks with industrial chic, because wood is warm and organic. Keep the doors plain with steel handles, and avoid drawers above cupboards if you can. A set of drawers on their own are actually more practical, and the look is more contemporary.

Floating wooden strip floor
This is laid on top of the existing floor—what could be simpler? All that's needed is a dry, level surface, a polystyrene sheet underlay and enough laminated floorboards to fit the room. The boards come in a range of wood finishes and the quality will be reflected in the price, which, with luck, includes a free fitting.

Frosted glass shelves
Frosted glass is cool. Use the reinforced version for shelves, supported by stainless steel brackets, as panels in doors, or design and make your own frosted window with painter's tape, templates, and etching spray.

Limited color range
When it comes to choosing color, think pale and interesting. Bright white is too stark and reflective, but pale grey, off-white, duck-egg blue or light sea green all suit this look. For a subtle

toned effect, pick a color and its immediate neighbors on the chart. Try and avoid strong contrasts, and go for harmonies instead.

Slatted blinds

Blinds provide the neatest window treatment but only if they fit perfectly and work efficiently. Roller blinds are neat and good value, but the ideal blind for this look is the slatted Venetian blind. Aluminum or light wood both look fabulous, and you can adjust them in several ways to filter the incoming light.

No clutter on worktops

The no-clutter rule has to be strictly enforced if this look is to succeed! Real life is not a clutter-free zone, and the only way to achieve this is by being very organized, with good storage and a place for everything. Lighten the look with fresh flowers, or a row of herbs in matching pots.

Chrome rails with matching utensils

Utensils don't belong in drawers, but they do need to be visible and well within reach. The best way to arrange them is by hanging them on a fitted rail above the worktop. This type of rail with hooks can be bought in a range of lengths and styles, or follow the simple instructions in the project and make your own.

Contemporary kitchen table and matching set of chairs or stools

The table is not the main attraction in a contemporary kitchen. A small, round, café-style table, or a simple foldaway version is a good idea, especially in small spaces, and avoid cluttering the no-frills look. Chairs are now very much in fashion, and there are so many new designs to choose from. Whether you go for lightweight, cast aluminum chairs, smooth beech with chrome

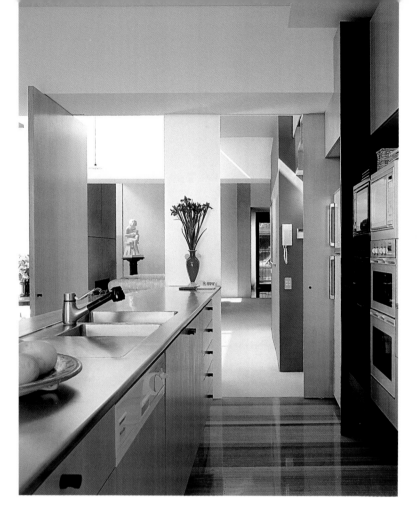

legs, or folding metal and polypropylene in jelly colors, it is hard to go wrong.

Recessed downlights in ceiling, or halogen spotlights

To see what you're doing in the kitchen, a combination of good task lighting and an ambient glow is ideal. Recessed ceiling lights look great, but there are restrictions on their use. Better still, use strip lights fitted below the wall cupboards, or you could opt for a row of halogen spotlights angled to illuminate the work area.

Worktops are kept clutter-free in a contemporary kitchen, so good storage space and planning a place for everything is a must.

THE PROJECTS
The three projects on the following pages will help you achieve a contemporary background in your own kitchen. A few stainless steel accessories, a fresh coat of paint, and some halogen lighting will do the rest.

YOU WILL NEED:

- READY-MADE DOOR OR A SHEET OF BEECH-FACED MDF
- SANDPAPER (IF YOU ARE MAKING A NEW DOOR)
- STEEL DOOR HANDLE WITH SCREWS
- NEW SPRING-LOADED HINGES (ONLY IF THE OLD ONES NEED REPLACING)
- SCREWDRIVER
- SCREWS
- $\frac{1}{8}$-IN. DRILL BIT
- DRILL
- 1 $\frac{3}{8}$-IN. SPADE BIT (IF YOU ARE RE-FITTING CONCEALED HINGES)
- PENCIL
- SPIRIT LEVEL

PROJECT ONE

Replacing existing doors

A change of doors on the kitchen units is one of the quickest ways to create a new look. Fitted kitchen units are made to a standard size and, although the hinges look quite complex, they are not difficult to fit. Ready-made hardwood doors are widely available, and it makes sense to use them if the style is right. The other option is to make them yourself using beech-faced MDF. You get the best of both worlds with a material like this. The MDF backing makes it easy to work with, and the beech facing has all the beauty of the natural grain. You can buy it from most good lumber merchants in sheets measuring 48 x 96 in. in a standard ¾-in. thickness.

Replacing kitchen unit doors is one of the quickest ways to create a new look. Because fitted kitchen units are made to a standard size, you can buy them ready-made. Add chrome handles to complete the look.

HOW TO DO IT

STEP 1 Support the door as you unscrew the hinges to remove it. If the screws are in a good condition, save them to re-use in the new door.

STEP 2 If you are making a new door, then use the old one as a template to draw around. Check the right angles and the measurements, and then cut out the new door with a handsaw and sandpaper the edges.

STEP 3 Mark the positions for the hinge fittings, and drill out the recess with the spade bit.

STEP 4 Hold the door in position with the hinge mechanism fitted into the recess, and mark the screw positions. Drill small pilot holes.

STEP 5 Screw the hinges to the doors. The fit of the door can be adjusted using the two screws on the hinge inside the cupboard. Loosen the screws, move the door slightly, and re-tighten them. Repeat this sequence until the fit is perfect.

STEP 6 Measure the positions for the screws or bolts accurately. The handles on all the doors must be perfectly aligned, so double-check and use a spirit level. Drill holes for the screws or bolts, and fit the handles.

YOU WILL NEED:

• STEEL OR CHROME
ROD WITH HOOKS (OR
TWO CHROME TOWEL
RAIL HOLDERS AND A
LENGTH OF RAIL)

• STRAIGHT EDGE
WITH A BUILT-IN
SPIRIT LEVEL

• PAINTER'S TAPE IF
THE WALL IS TILED

• DRILL

• CORRECT SIZE
MASONRY DRILL
BIT FOR THE SCREWS
(EG SCREW SIZE No. 6,
BIT SIZE No. 6)

• WALL ANCHORS FOR
A BRICK WALL (OR
CAVITY WALL
ANCHORS FOR
WALLBOARD)

PROJECT TWO

Fitting a chrome utensil rod to the wall

The first thing you need to discover is what your wall is made of. The usual suspects are painted or tiled brick or wallboard, and they require different wall fixings. There is also a knack to drilling holes in tiles successfully. Use a small strip of painter's tape that has to be placed on the tile before you mark the screw position. The tape stops the drill bit from skidding off as it spins. Whether you buy a ready-made rod or make one yourself by customizing a chrome towel rod, the actual task of fitting it to the wall will be the same.

Chrome utensil rods can be bought ready-made, or you can make them by customizing a chrome towel rod. When you are deciding which height to fit it, hang the longest utensil from the rod to make sure it's high enough.

HOW TO DO IT

STEP 1 Decide where you would like the rod on the wall. Do this with the longest of the utensils hanging from it. Place strips of painter's tape on the tiles roughly where holes need to be drilled.

STEP 2 Hold up the rod to the wall with the spirit level. Make certain that the rod is level, then accurately mark the positions for the screws. Drill the holes for the wall anchors. Hold the drill at a right angle to the wall and apply firm pressure as you drill.

TIPS
• Chrome rods can be clamped to a workbench or a table edge, and cut down to size with a hacksaw.
• Wooden doweling rods can be used with chrome towel rod fittings to give a softer look. They are especially suitable if you have wooden floors or cupboard doors.
• Buy butcher-style hooks, without sharp points, from kitchenware stores.

STEP 3 Push the anchors into the holes, tapping them lightly with a hammer if necessary. They should fit snugly and stay in place. If the hole is too big you may need to go up a size with both wall anchors and screws.

STEP 4 Screw in the top screw on each side to support the rod as you tighten the other screws.

YOU WILL NEED:
• SCREWDRIVER
• WOOD FILLER
• SANDPAPER
• SET OF NEW HANDLES
• SPIRIT LEVEL
• DRILL FITTED WITH
  A BIT TO MATCH THE
  BOLT SIZE

PROJECT THREE

Changing handles

This is an easy project to provide an instant lift. Fashions change, thank goodness, and at the moment knobs are out and long, thin steel handles are in. They are usually fixed with bolts that screw in from the back of the door. It is a style that only suits plain doors and drawers because the look emphasizes clean lines and good design. If you have doors with moldings and panels, then consider replacing the doors altogether, or facing them with hardboard or ¼-in. MDF stuck down with panel adhesive.

Fitting new handles on kitchen units provides an instant lift. Long, thin steel handles emphasize clean lines, so they only suit plain doors.

HOW TO DO IT

STEP 1 Unscrew the old handles or knobs, and fill the holes. When the filler has dried, sand it flat, and touch up the paint or varnish. You may decide to take this opportunity to refresh all the paintwork, but that is another story.

STEP 2 Decide on the position for the new handle. This can be fitted horizontally or vertically about 1 in. from the door edge—both ways look good. Check it with the spirit level, then mark the fitting positions.

TIPS
• If you are changing the handles on a row of units, it is vital to fit them in a straight line. Make a cardboard template with the bolt positions drilled out. This can be placed against the back of each cupboard to make sure that the handle positions do not vary.

STEP 3 Drill the holes for the bolts. Check each hole against the next mark with the spirit level before you drill the hole.

STEP 4 Tighten the screws or bolts from the back of the door; you can hold the handles if it makes it easier.

The 1950s kitchen
Sometimes it seems that color was invented in the 1950s, because everything before that was photographed in black and white. In truth, homes were pretty dull during the war years, but it was also a time of great advances in technology and design. When all the brainpower and new materials were no longer needed for the war effort, thoughts turned toward the commercial world.

Formica worktops are a key element in any 1950s-style kitchen, along with contrasting colors, such as primrose yellow used with black. Streamlined, rocket-shaped bins and other appliances complete the look.

The 1950s kitchen is a part of the American dream, fitted with bright Formica worktops, shiny chrome appliances, colorful plastics, and checked lino flooring. It started in America, but the look took off across the Atlantic as soon as it was seen in those Doris Day movies. Keep an eye out for 1950s cookery books in thrift shops or secondhand bookstores because they offer a wealth of inspiration. Genuine 1950s kitchen units are collectors' items now, but you can still pick up kitchen accessories in junk stores and specialized stores. The 1950s revival is always simmering away on the back burner, and kitchen furniture with that look features in many contemporary ranges, mixing chrome, leather, Formica, and fun. The top 10 ingredients that make the 1950s style kitchen are…

Rounded, streamlined steel, and chrome appliances
The streamlined style was inspired by the advent of the jet plane and excitement surrounding space rocket missions. Sleek chrome striping was used to make stationary kitchen appliances look as though they were speeding! Everything from fridges to food mixers were given this look, and some of the best designs are still in production today. Look out for reconditioned refridgerators and repro toasters, chrome bins, kettles, blenders, kitchen clocks, and radios. Because they are still a popular style, they shouldn't be hard to find.

Red and white checkerboard vinyl floor
Some of the least expensive floor tiles on the market are slightly marbleized, self-adhesive, plain-colored vinyl. They have the look of authentic 1950s lino, but at a fraction of the cost. Go for a big color contrast—red and white, or yellow and black checkerboard floors may not appeal to the faint-hearted, but when you see them reflected in the chromework—wow!

Small black-and-white checkered borders
Small, black-and-white checkered borders seen on the sides of New York taxicabs often feature in 1950s-style diners. There are two ways to get the same effect without re-tiling the kitchen: one is to apply the checkerboard pattern on a self-adhesive tape strip, and the other is to print the border with a rubber roller stamp, bought from a specialized crafts supplier.

Walls painted in contrasting colors
Color in the 1950s was all about contrasts. Pale colors like eau de nil (a light green), or primrose yellow and sky blue were often used with black. And you can't fail with red, whether it's just the plastic handles of cupboards and drawers or a whole wall painted in red enamel. Different-colored walls, or blocks of strong color on a part of a pale wall are the look to go for.

Patterns—polka dots and stars

One of the most popular patterns for wallpaper in the 1950s had small white stars or spots on a colored background that would be used on just one wall. Tablecloths and curtains were made from polka-dot fabric reversed out, where the pattern color swapped over with the background color.

Formica

Formica is the plastic laminate that revolutionized kitchen worktops. It is one of the key elements in any 1950s-style kitchen. Choose bright yellow, cherry red, or sky blue for a big impact, and take it up the wall behind the worktop as a splashback.

Tubular steel

If you ever see a set of old, chromed-steel kitchen chairs then buy them, regardless of the state of the upholstery. Re-cover the seats with soft vinyl stapled in place, edged with a row of chrome upholstery studs. These retro-style kitchen tables and chairs are back in fashion and are really expensive, so cheat if you possibly can.

Kitsch

Kitsch is the German word for bad taste, but sometimes bad taste is actually good taste, especially when it is entirely deliberate! Think of Elvis in *Blue Hawaii*, with plastic fruit and flowers, sunsets, neon signs, flying ducks, laminated calendars, and anything plastic in the shape of a poodle!

THE PROJECTS
The three projects on the following pages will help you achieve a 1950s background in your own kitchen. A few kitsch accessories, some streamlined chrome appliances, and some black-and-white checkered borders will do the rest.

Colorful modern ceramics

Organic shapes, Picasso-inspired patterns, and bright contrasting colors give 1950s ceramics a highly distinctive look. These things are within everyone's budget, so get out there and start looking. Try inexpensive yard sales and junk stores, but if you can't spare the time to trawl, find a trader who specializes in 1950s ware.

Packaging and plastics

Quite a lot of cheap plastic ware manufactured in the Far East fits in well with this look. American mustard in a bright yellow squeezy bottle, or a large plastic tomato filled with ketchup helps to set the scene. You do have to be selective, but that is the fun of putting a themed look together.

Checkerboard vinyl floors can be bought as self-adhesive tiles at a fraction of the cost of authentic 1950s lino. The bigger the contrast in colors the better.

PROJECT ONE
Painting the kitchen units

The idea that melamine kitchen units can be painted is actually quite new. This has a lot to do with TV makeover programs and the popularity of home-style magazines. Once the makeover idea took off, people started experimenting, trying different products and discovering new uses for old materials.

The problem with a shiny surface like melamine is that, without the right primer, the paint has nothing to key into and is easily scratched. The trick is to scratch the surface with a silicone-carbide sandpaper, then apply one or two coats of a shellac-based primer. It gives good coverage, is very strong, and leaves an ultra-matte surface.

Go creative on your kitchen units! Melamine kitchen units can be painted, so long as they are prepared beforehand, using sandpaper to scratch the surface and primer to give an ultra-matte surface.

HOW TO DO IT

STEP 1 Clean the doors with a grease-cutting detergent or abrasive powder. Rub them down with silicone-carbide sandpaper to remove the shine from the surface.

STEP 2 Apply the primer with the roller and leave to dry (repeat if necessary). Apply the main color (repeat if necessary).

STEP 3 Enlarge the two stencil patterns and transfer them onto a stencil card or plastic. Cut them out with a snap-blade knife. Paint the background shapes first in the light color.

STEP 4 Use the second stencil to apply the pattern inside the shapes, and then apply two coats of clear enamel varnish.

Enlarge the stencils and transfer them onto plastic or stencil paper. The guides to the left will help you position the two main stencils together on your kitchen unit door.

PROJECT TWO

Fitting a stainless steel, zinc, or aluminum splashback

Measure the size of the splashback area, then visit a sheet metal merchant. They cut metal sheets to size, and will usually have a stock of off-cuts suitable for small jobs like this. Explain what you will be using it for, and check that the type you have chosen will keep its shine and never rust. They have the right equipment, so ask for the sheet to be cut to size and for the edges to be buffed. There may be a charge for this service, but it will be worth it!

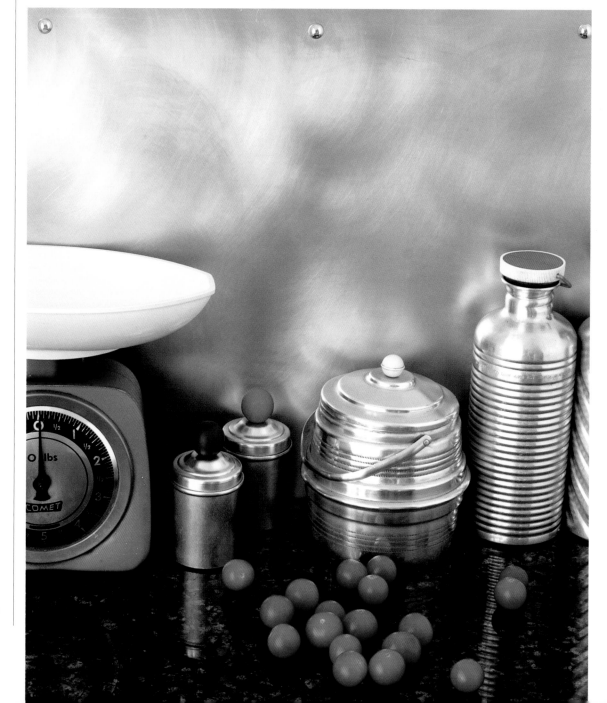

Metal sheets can be bought as off-cuts from a sheet metal merchant and cut to size with the edges buffed. You can drill holes in the sheet using the same bit as you use for wood.

HOW TO DO IT

STEP 1 Measure the splashback area. Don't have it too narrow, because it needs to be about one-third of the depth of the worktop. Mark the positions of the screws with a center punch.

STEP 2 Holes can be drilled in sheet metal using the same bit as you use for wood. You will need to have a wall fixing approximately every 1 in. on a long strip. Drill all the screw holes in the metal, and then hold it in position as you mark the screw positions on the wall.

TIP
• Perspex is a more colorful option. Shopfitters use it and will cut it to size.

STEP 3 Drill the screw holes in the wall then push in the wall anchors. If you are fitting this on a solid wall use regular wall anchors, but for wallboard you need cavity wall anchors that grip from the back.

STEP 4 Place the splashback against the wall and screw it in place. Screw the domed caps into the screw heads.

YOU WILL NEED:
- ³/₄-IN. MDF
- JIGSAW
- HACKSAW
- WORKBENCH
  OR TABLE WITH
  2 C–CLAMPS
- STICKY-BACK
  PLASTIC (OR FORMICA
  AND PANEL ADHESIVE)
- WOODEN SUPPORT
  BRACKETS
- CHROME CARPET-
  FITTING STRIP

PROJECT THREE

Creating a breakfast bar

The breakfast bar is just the thing for informal snacking. It is the very place to perch on a stool as you munch your toast and sip your espresso, or for a friend to have a drink while watching you cook. The 1950s styling means that you can have fun with the shape and cover it with shiny Formica or sticky-back plastic sheeting, whichever the budget allows.

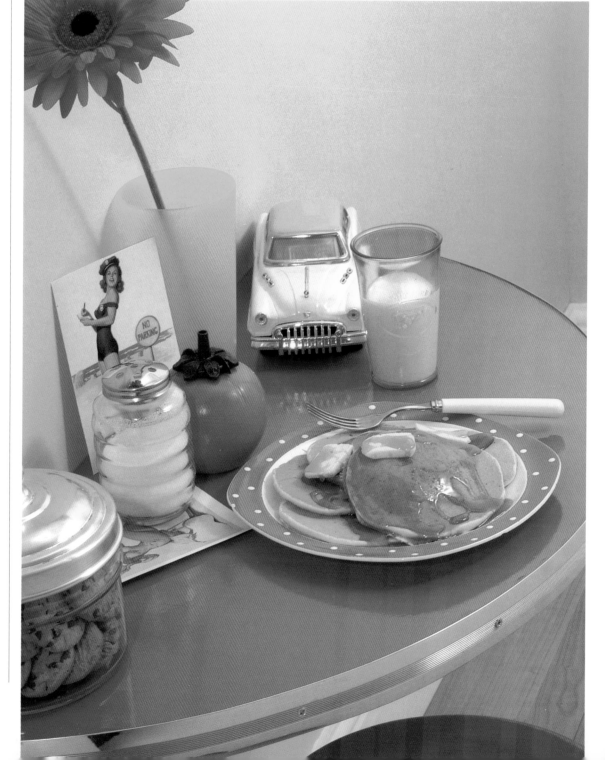

Breakfast bars make a convenient and space-saving place to have a snack, and this 1950s-style version is fun and colorful. It can be made out of MDF and covered with Formica or sticky-back plastic sheeting.

HOW TO DO IT

STEP 1 Draw out the shape of the pattern on the MDF. Cut the pattern out with a jigsaw. Hold the jigsaw firmly down on the surface and move with it. Sand the edge smooth, then wipe away any dust with a damp cloth.

STEP 2 Cover the MDF with sticky-back plastic, smoothing it flat as you roll it on. Snip notches on the curve of the table, and fold over the edge so the plastic lays flat.

STEP 3 Cut the chrome carpet-fitting strip to size with a hacksaw.

STEP 4 Drill pilot holes for the chrome strip and then into place on the edge of the table. Begin at one end of the curve, bending the strip as you go.

STEP 5 Drill holes for the bracket fittings in both the wall and MDF. Mark the position for the fittings on the wall, and drill the holes. Fit the appropriate wall anchors into the holes.

STEP 6 Screw the brackets to the wall first, then screw them to the MDF. Trim the edge. Use a spirit level to check.

Check these illustrations when you are constructing and attaching the brackets to your kitchen wall. Always double-check that they are straight with a spirit level.

Galley kitchen

A small kitchen space should be seen as a challenge and not a problem. Believe it or not, squeezing everything into an area the size of a corridor can be an easier task than putting together a coherent style in acres of space. By using storage solutions that make the best use of the space available, galley kitchens can look extremely stylish.

Stools are an ideal seating choice for galley kitchens because, although they may take up the same area of floor space as chairs, their height makes them less dense and claustrophobic.

Start by evaluating what you have in the way of major appliances, such as the cooker, refrigerator, freezer, washing machine, and tumble dryer. Some may be too big, and some you may not need at all. Do you only ever half-fill the refrigerator and freezer? Do you cook only under the grill, in the microwave, or on the hob, and would a mini-oven be better? And do you really need a washing machine and tumble dryer? Compact versions that are more in line with your lifestyle will certainly save a lot of space and money on fuel bills. Also make sure that all the kitchen's storage potential is being used, and that there is no "dead" space. Only keep essential equipment, and make sure that the things you use most are stored within easy reach. Remember, a galley kitchen must be functional, with as much floor space as possible, and easily accessed cupboards and appliances. A long, thin kitchen can afford to have the space trimmed down a bit and fitted with wall-to-wall shelving around the door frame. Worktops need to be kept clutter free with the food and crockery hidden behind doors.

Gentle variations in color, or using the same color for worktops, walls, and units, will make the space seem bigger, and brushed steel appliances and shiny splashbacks can help by reflecting light. There is so much that can be done with a can of paint, and the new, multi-surface paints have extended these boundaries even further.

A number of important points to consider when kitchen space is tight are…

Sliding or folding doors

A door opening into a galley kitchen will be using up quite a lot of space. One way of reclaiming space is to have the door re-hung so that it opens the other way, and another is to fit a sliding door on the outside. Sliding doors still need somewhere to slide to, and if you don't have this space then think about a folding door. Concertina-style melamine panels with steel hinges look sleek, and take up only the space of the door area. Or you could make up a double-sided, heavy-duty PVC curtain with eyelets, and thread it onto a chrome tube rail.

Glass shelves over windows

Kitchen windows are usually quite a generous size, which means that they eat up potential wall and storage space. If this is your problem, section off part of the window and fit it with glass shelves. The space above a window is an ideal place to store your glassware, because the natural light is not completely blocked, and glasses can sparkle within easy reach.

Plain flooring

Since the overall floor area of a galley kitchen is fairly small, it should not cost the earth to invest in some very flattering floor covering. All patterned flooring follows a repeat grid of some type, and the grid pattern will visually "shrink" the floor space. Instead, choose a floating, wooden strip floor laid crosswise, or plain-colored sheet lino or vinyl flooring.

Glass and brushed steel surfaces reflect light around a galley kitchen, helping create a bigger sense of space.

Storage—everywhere

Make full use of every bit of space. Kitchen units are made to a standard depth, but most of us have things lurking toward the back that never see the light of day. Reduce the cupboard depth by 6 in., and you might have room to swing that cat! Create even more space in a shallow cupboard by fitting two shelves instead of one, to make full use of the height. Fit a row of wall cupboards above eye level for things you use less often.

Task lighting

Draw the eye toward the action by lighting the worktops with an angled track of halogen spotlights. A small kitchen is no place to be stumbling about in the dark with hot oil, so make sure the work areas are bright when you need them to be. It is also best to have an ambient light source to soften the effect. Recessed, dimmable ceiling lights or even a stylish table lamp will allow for a change of atmosphere when you want it.

Expanding space with color

When decorating a small room, it is best to work with a limited palette. Use one main color with perhaps a darker and lighter version. Earth colors work well if you have wooden doors and floors, blue is a receding color and will "expand" the space, and bold, bright yellow is good with metal. Red will make the room look smaller but

quite sexy, and white will dazzle. If you need to reflect natural light with pale walls, choose cream because it looks delicious with dark wood.

Foldaway counters

Think of trailers or yachts because they provide plenty of practical inspiration for the galley kitchen. Fold-down flaps, collapsible tables, high cupboards like airplane lockers, and pull-out breadboards are all good ideas to adapt with a touch of contemporary styling.

Stools instead of chairs

Chairs and stool legs may take up roughly the same area of floor space, but stools are less claustrophobic in galley kitchens. Perched on a high stool looking down on the worktops, the view is of the widest part of the kitchen.

Homely touches

Never forget that this galley kitchen is part of your home. Design tips can help you make the best of the space, but you should always feel free to introduce your personal style. Efficiently designed kitchens can look too clinical, so be sure to introduce some homely touches.

THE PROJECTS

The three projects on the following pages are practical, space-saving solutions that will help optimize the space in your own galley kitchen. Think about adding a few homely touches of your own to personalize the effect.

PROJECT ONE

Making a hinged breakfast bar

When space is limited, it is worth thinking about when and how the room is used. There is no need to allot precious space to a permanent eating area if it is only going to be used for a quick croissant and coffee in the morning, or a bowl of noodles at night.

A foldaway bar like this one is ideal in this situation, and if you make one to match the color of the kitchen walls, it will virtually disappear when it's not in use. Alternatively, you could choose to make a feature of it and cover it with a bright color or pattern.

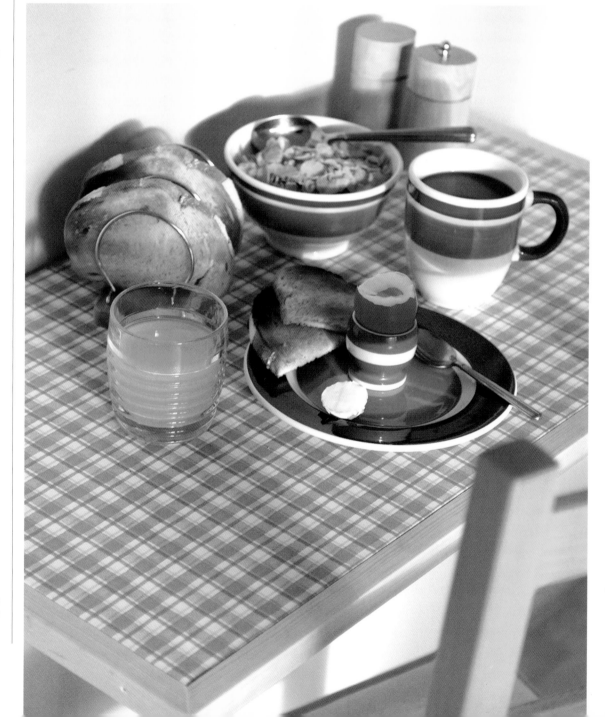

Wall-mounted, hinged breakfast bars are ideal eating areas that can be folded away after use.

HOW TO DO IT

STEP 1 Cut the MDF to the size required and cover with sticky-back plastic, snipping and folding the corners to make a neat edge.

STEP 2 Cut and miter the molding, and use brads to attach it to the MDF. Use a center punch to punch the brads home.

STEP 3 Determine the position of the shelf on the wall, using a tape measure and pencil.

STEP 4 Place the shortest end of the bracket on the wall and mark screw positions. Fix and tighten all the screws.

STEP 5 Align the second bracket with the spirit level. Check the horizontal. Fix the second bracket as described in step 4.

STEP 6 Fix the shelf to the brackets, leaving a ³/₁₆-in. gap between the wall and the shelf for easy folding.

TIPS
• Drill a pilot hole using a ¹/₈-in. drill bit if you are screwing into MDF.
• Give up painting furniture with brushes and use small "enamel" rollers instead. The finish is far better and you avoid the drips.
• Design the breakfast bar as an extension to the kitchen worktop, so long as it doesn't block a cupboard door when folded down.

YOU WILL NEED:

• LUMBER AS FOLLOWS
4 LEGS 2 x 2 IN.,
23 IN. LONG;
4 FEET 1 ⅝-IN.
WOODEN KNOBS
WITH SCREWS;
1 BOX BASE ½-IN.
MDF, 12 x 12 IN.;
2 BOX SIDES ½-IN.
MDF, 12 x 8 IN.;
2 BOX SIDES ½-IN.
MDF, 13 x 8 IN.;
2 SEAT FRAMES ½-IN.
MDF, 12 x 31½ IN.;
2 SEAT FRAMES ½-IN.
MDF, 13 x 31½ IN.;
1 SEAT 1-IN. MDF,
14 x 14 IN.
• PENCIL
• TAPE MEASURE
• STRAIGHT EDGE
• SAW
• WOOD GLUE
• DRILL WITH 1⅝-IN.
BIT AND
COUNTERSUNK BIT
• BOX OF 1⅝-IN.
No. 6 SCREWS
• PRIMER
• PAINT
• SMALL FOAM ROLLER
AND TRAY

PROJECT TWO
Stools for storage

Remember the space rule, and don't waste an inch of it. This high stool is easy for a beginner to make, and has a useful storage box in the base. The stool can be painted to match the kitchen if you want it to blend in, or try primary colors with black legs for a Bauhaus look.

Not an inch is wasted by this high stool, which has a storage box in the base. Experiment with colors that either match or contrast with the rest of the kitchen.

HOW TO DO IT

STEP 1 Make up the two shorter sides. Drill, countersink, glue, and screw the 12-in. seat frame across the top of each pair of legs. Check that the legs are square to the seat.

STEP 2 Drill, countersink, glue, and screw the 12-in. box sides at the other end to overlap the ends of the legs by ½ in., and allow for the depth of the box base. Check that everything is square!

STEP 3 Join the two sides of the stool by fixing the 13-in. seat base and box sides between them.

STEP 4 Fix the base by screwing up into the legs from below. If this is a nice, tight fit, it will add stability. Fix the seat on from the top.

STEP 5 Fill all the countersunk holes with wood filler, leave to set, and then sand smooth. Prime and paint the stool using a small foam roller.

STEP 6 Drill four pilot holes, then screw the wooden feet into the base.

TIPS
• You might need to plane a small amount of wood from the underneath of each of the wooden knobs that are to be used as feet. Check how the stool stands on the floor, and adjust the feet accordingly.

YOU WILL NEED:
- HOOKS
- DRILL
- PILOT 1/8-IN. BIT
- SCREWDRIVER
- MITER BLOCK
- BACKSAW
- 12 IN. OF 2 X 2 IN. LUMBER FOR SUPPORTS
- 7/8-IN. SPADE BIT
- 7/8-IN. COPPER PIPE

PROJECT THREE

Fitting a rod below a floating shelf

Shelves with internal brackets give the kitchen a contemporary edge, and by fitting steel rods for cups below the shelf you can double its usefulness. If you are displaying glasses, cups, or mugs in this way invest in a brand new matching set so that you can enjoy looking at them. Buy the shelves from a hardware store: they will have full

fitting instructions and the fixings needed to complete the job. The design of the steel rod is best kept simple—as a rule the cheaper they are, the more elaborate —so shop around for a rail that pleases the eye. Some of them can be bought with hooks, if not, buy blunt "S" hooks rather than butcher's hooks, which have lethal points.

Open shelves fitted with steel rods provide useful storage space without blocking out areas of the galley kitchen. Matching sets of crockery are preferable to odd sets, if you are putting them on display.

HOW TO DO IT

STEP 1 Use the backsaw and miter block to cut the supports for the rail.

STEP 2 Use the ⅞-in. spade bit to drill holes in the supports to take the rail. Drill to ⅝-in. depth.

STEP 3 Drill a pilot hole through the shelf, and screw the first support in place.

STEP 4 Fit the pipe into the hole of the fixed support, and then fit the second support at the other end of the shelf. Screw this in position from above.

Sitting rooms

The sitting room is a space to relax, to read, and to watch television. It is also the place to entertain visitors, so, as the most public face of your home, it is an ideal room to reflect your personal style. This section shows you how to transform your sitting room into a choice of three different styles: Traditional, Contemporary, or Global. Most sizes and shapes of sitting rooms can achieve one of these three styles, but an additional section shows you how to make the most of a small sitting room. The three step-by-step projects will start you off, and a few accessories and a fresh coat of paint will do the rest.

Traditional sitting room

The traditional sitting room is a comfort zone. A place to relax alone or with company, perhaps watch TV or listen to music, to curl up with a magazine or a good book and warm your toes in front of the open fire— somewhere to feel at home. If you live in an old building, the shape and height of the room probably suggest that you decorate it in a traditional way. Begin by choosing the right colors. Most paint companies now have a range of historical colors that are suited to different decorative periods. You don't have to recreate the past, but getting the colors right can make a huge difference to a room.

Comfortable sofas, colorful rugs, and a generous scattering of cushions make the traditional sitting room a comfort zone.

The great thing now is that we have so much choice, not only in color schemes but also in lighting, furniture, and accessories. Gas-fuelled open fires are more realistic than ever, and whether you're after chandeliers or gilded mirrors, you will find excellent reproduction versions in department stores or the genuine article in antique markets. If it's out there somewhere, there will very likely be a directory to help you find it.

One very good reason for decorating a sitting room in a traditional style is that you can mix old and new pieces of furniture. Furniture is passed down through families, and whether they are priceless antiques or simply granny's standard lamp, they give a home a sense of history. And if the idea of granny's lamp fills you with horror, remember it can always be repainted and treated to a new lampshade. Comfortable old sofas can be re-upholstered or dressed up with colorful throws and cushions. Try mixing old with new, even if you have to cheat and buy your "family heirlooms" from a flea market. They are often exactly what a traditionally decorated sitting room needs to settle it down, and turn it into that comfort zone. Ten points to consider that will help you to get the look are…

Open fireplace

There was a time when fireplaces were boarded up because they were too old-fashioned for the modern home. They were soon opened up, however, because sitting rooms seemed so much colder and less inviting without them. If you have the real thing, dress it up with a full log basket, a coal bucket, and a range of fire implements. Victorian and 1900s-style fireplaces are still made from the original designs, and today some of them don't even need a chimney. They can be gas fuelled and lit from the comfort of your armchair via a remote control!

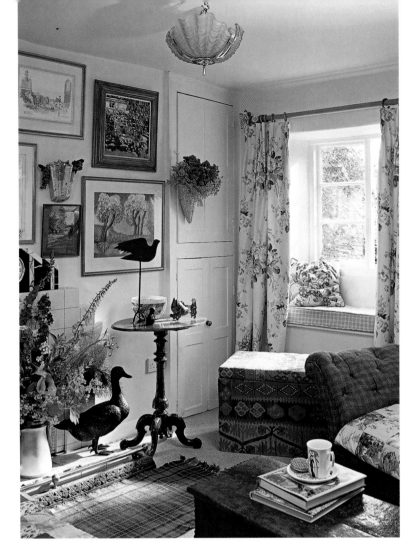

Fitted carpets

A traditional sitting room can have polished floorboards with a scattering of rugs or good old fitted carpets. Hard floors are fashionable at the moment, but you really can't beat wall-to-wall carpets for warmth and comfort. Choose a warm, neutral color, or a woven natural material like seagrass or coir matting that matches most furniture styles.

Armchairs

There are lots of comfortable armchairs that look pretty dreadful, and fabulous-looking armchairs that weren't meant to be sat in. You should strike a balance, but looks must come into the equation. A brand new armchair can cost almost as much as a sofa, so look out for a secondhand bargain. Give an old chair new life by re-upholstering it to suit the rest of the furniture.

Rugs and cushions

Rugs are like pictures on the floor. They don't have to cost a fortune, but can become the focal point in a room. Plain floors can be brightened up with splashes of color, and rugs also provide soft islands of comfort on hard, wooden floors. Cushions do the same job on furniture. Don't be mean with them—the more the merrier!

Throws

Throws are not really a new invention, they are just blankets with a new name. We have all been liberated by them, though, no doubt about it! Before the throw came along, there was no alternative but to send for the steam cleaners or to re-upholster when accidents happened, but now we chuck on a throw and hide a multitude of sins. Throws can also introduce strong, contrasting colors, and create a more casual, relaxed, and informal look.

Curtains

"Grown-up" curtains can be terribly expensive, and choosing the fabric is the only exciting part of the experience. The linings, weights, tracks, and hooks are not at all thrilling, and they can be seriously expensive. This does explain the popularity of curtain poles and tab-tops, which are simplicity itself to put up. Buy them ready-made for convenience, or buy fabric and make them yourself. If you still long for a serious set of curtains, there are specialized secondhand curtain dealers who are not cheap, but you do get totally authentic grandeur.

Framed photographs, paintings, and prints

Traditional sitting rooms need art on the walls. This gives you something to look at while you

The traditional sitting room mixes the old with the new, so it is an ideal place to arrange your family heirlooms (even if you have to cheat and buy them from a flea market).

them actually flatter the room. It is difficult to get the proportions right, and the light is very often far too bright, which creates a stark atmosphere. Large table lamps are better all round. They can sit on tables and cast a warm glow onto the seating area. Picture lights or wall uplighters can be used to supply more ambient light to the room.

Comfortable sofas

There are so many cheap sofas and special offers in the stores, but for the traditional look it makes more sense to wait until sale time and spend as much as possible on a quality piece of furniture in a traditional design, such as a Chesterfield. If you don't mind buying secondhand, it is worth checking out local furniture auctions. They can be great fun, and you never know what you might find. Factory outlets are also worth investigating, because many sell end-of-lines and uncollected special orders at knock-down prices.

Bookshelves

Restaurants, bars, and hotels have recently caught on to the fact that rows of books make the place feel like home. Fit a row of shelves into an alcove, and make a display of your books. You can cheat a bit as well—think of them as accessories and buy sets of secondhand books for their bindings. Book spines can be very decorative, and thrift shops always have loads of hardcovers to choose from.

Wall uplighters and large table lamps are far better methods of lighting than central ceiling lights. They cast a warm, ambient light over the room.

are relaxing, and to talk about when friends drop by. Don't worry if you don't know your Picasso from your Leonardo, you can always cheat a little. Buy old frames from a flea market and revitalize them with gilding cream or an antique gold spray paint. Frame mirrors, prints, photocopied drawings or etchings, old black-and-white photographs, and don't forget to keep a lookout for an original masterpiece.

Lighting

Most sitting rooms have central lights that hang down from the ceiling, but very few of

THE PROJECTS
The four projects on the following pages will help achieve a traditional feel to your own sitting room by adding soft, cozy furnishings on top of your existing items. Some old-framed mirrors and prints with some warm lighting will do the rest.

YOU WILL NEED:
- 2 CONTRASTING PIECES OF FABRIC ABOUT 60 IN. SQUARE (IF THE FABRIC IS TOO NARROW, STITCH 2 WIDTHS TOGETHER AND USE THIS MEASUREMENT FOR THE LENGTH AS WELL)
- TAPE MEASURE
- SCISSORS
- PINS
- SEWING MACHINE
- THREAD
- EDGE TRIMMING

PROJECT ONE

Throws

A throw is quite simply the most versatile of all soft furnishings. Throws are usually square, but there are no size or fabric restrictions. When it comes to throws, anything goes! Make a double-thickness throw using fabrics with contrasting textures and colors. This could be velvet and corduroy, fleece and cotton, or perhaps a color co-ordinated patterned or plain fabric. Add extra style around the edge with a fringed, beaded, or blanket-stitched border.

A new throw is a cheap and easy way to transform an elderly sofa or armchair, and can add a splash of warm color to the sitting room.

HOW TO DO IT

STEP 1 Trim the patterned fabric so it is 2 in. smaller than the plain fabric. Pin the two pieces together. Miter the corners.

STEP 2 Sew a double row of stitches about 5/8 in. in from the edge, but leave a 1 1/8 in. opening in the middle of one side. Turn the fleece over to form a border, and zigzag the two together along the joining edge.

TIPS
- A dark-colored brushed cotton sheet is soft and wide, and makes a good lining fabric.
- If you have never sewn with fleece, try it! It is wide, inexpensive, the edges don't fray, it washes brilliantly, and comes in a fabulous range of colors.
- Good decorative touches include tassels, buttons, twisted cord, piping, or a beaded fringe.

PROJECT TWO

Cushions

A chair or sofa will always look more inviting if it's stacked with plumped-up cushions. Neutral, plain-colored covers for sofas and chairs are the most popular choice because furniture is a major expense and we want something that won't date. Cushions can be much more frivolous. A new cushion cover is quick, easy, and inexpensive to make, especially if you buy remnants of luxurious fabrics. These leftovers are sold at a fraction of the original price.

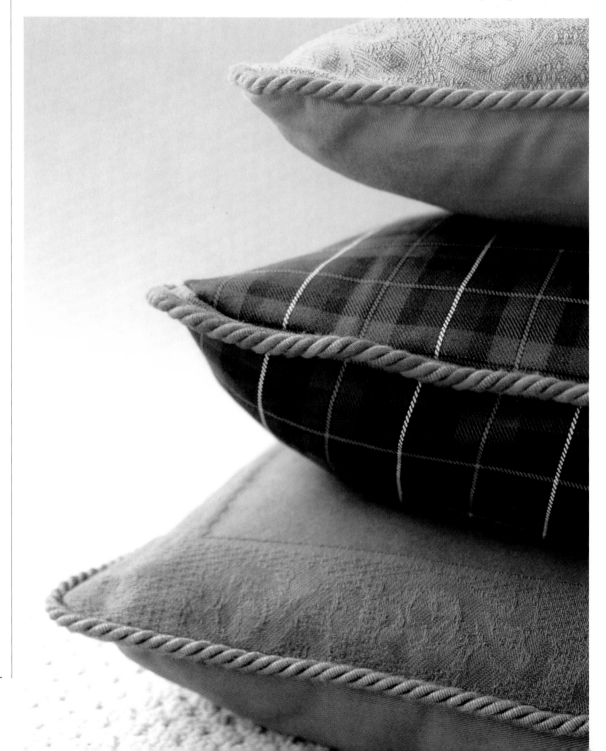

A splash of strong color on a neutral-colored sofa in the form of plumped-up cushions creates an inviting and cosy look.

HOW TO DO IT

STEP 1 Cut one square of fabric to be the front of the cushion. Cut two pieces to overlap each other at the back. These two must measure as wide as the first square, but only be two-thirds as long.

STEP 2 Turn back and zigzag a small hem along one edge of each of the smaller pieces. These two seams will overlap at the back of the cushion, making an "envelope" access for the cushion pad.

STEP 3 Lay the square flat with the right side facing upwards. Place the two shorter pieces face down on it, one at each end so that they overlap one another in the middle, with the hem-stitched edges facing upwards. Piped cord can also be sandwiched in at this stage, with the flat edge facing outward. Pin all round the edge.

STEP 4 Sew the pieces together, about ⅝ in. inside the outer edge. Turn the cushion cover the right side out and press with an iron. Place the cushion pad inside the cover. For most fabrics the overlap will not need any additional fixings, but soft, silky fabrics will hold their shape better with a press stud, ribbon tie, or Velcro dot attached inside the overlap.

PROJECT THREE
Curtain treatments

YOU WILL NEED:
- FABRIC (MEASURE THE HEIGHT OF YOUR WINDOW AND ADD 3 IN. FOR THE HEADER AND HEM, THEN MAKE EACH CURTAIN TO THE WIDTH OF THE FABRIC)
- LINING (THE SAME AMOUNT AS THE FEATURE FABRIC)
- SCISSORS
- TAPE MEASURE
- IRON-ON STIFFENER FOR HEADING AND TABS
- BUTTONS FOR THE TABS (OPTIONAL)
- SEWING MACHINE

Let the proportions of your room and the size of your windows be the deciding factor when you choose your curtain style. A large, high-ceilinged room with a bay window can look fabulous with a heavy valance and pleated drapes, but a smaller room would be overwhelmed by this sort of treatment and needs something lighter. A combination of plain blinds and fabric draped over a curtain pole can provide the best of both worlds. The window panes are covered by the blinds, while the hard lines of the frames are softened by the drapes.

If you have double glazing and don't need curtains for warmth, a curtain rod with ring clips is the quickest solution. The row of clips is snapped on at regular intervals and will hold most light-to-medium-weight fabrics. Sheets, saris, and even large tablecloths can make the most elegant curtains. The project shows how to make simple tab-top, banner-style curtains.

Tab-topped curtains give a lighter effect than valances and pleats, so they are ideal for slightly smaller rooms and windows. Choose between a wooden or iron pole.

HOW TO DO IT

STEP 1 Measure and cut out the curtain panels and matching lining. Tab tops do not need to be much wider than the actual window width because they hang almost flat when pulled. Cut out tabs 1 ⅛ in. wide and 4 ¾ in. long. Calculate how many you need, spacing them 6 in. apart. Cut out the same shape and number of strips of fabric stiffener, and iron it to the wrong side of the tabs. Iron a 2-in.-wide strip of stiffener to the wrong side of the top edge of each curtain panel.

STEP 2 Sew the tabs into tubes with the stiffener on the outside. Turn them inside out and press flat. Fold each tab in half along its length, and press.

STEP 3 Pin the sides and bottom lining and fabric together with the right sides facing. Stitch around the edge, and then fold the right way round. Turn the raw edges over at the top and tuck them inside. Space the folded tabs along the top edge and pin them to the stiffened fabric. Sew a double row of stitching across the top to close the seam and attach the tabs. Press the panels.

TIPS
• Stitch a button or wooden bead at the base of each loop.
• If you can't sew, buy iron-on tabs and press the seams with fabric-bonding tape.
• Paint a cheap curtain pole black, and use gold leaf or paint in bands to add a touch of glamor.

YOU WILL NEED:
- 1 X 2 IN. LUMBER FOR THE FRAMES
- TO MAKE A TWO-PANEL SCREEN 60 IN. TALL YOU NEED 44 FT. OF LUMBER, MITERED AS 2 3/8 X 60 IN. AND 2 3/8 X 30 IN.
- 4 SMALL DOOR KNOBS FOR FEET
- MITER SAW (OR BACKSAW AND MITER BLOCK)
- TAPE MEASURE
- PENCIL
- WOOD GLUE
- THIN PINS
- SMALL HAMMER
- 9 X TWO-WAY HINGES AND SCREWS TO FIT
- BRADAWL
- SCREWDRIVER

TO FILL EACH FRAME YOU NEED:
- PANEL OF HEAVY UPHOLSTERY FABRIC, TAPESTRY OR IKAT (TIE-DYED) STYLE
- STAPLE GUN
- WOOD PRIMER AND UNDERCOAT
- PAINT—SEMIGLOSS OR EGGSHELL FOR A MATTE FINISH
- SMALL ENAMEL ROLLER AND TRAY
- BRAID FOR TRIMMING
- FABRIC ADHESIVE

PROJECT FOUR

Making a two-panel screen to hide modern equipment

All your efforts to recreate the atmosphere of a traditional sitting room can be ruined by televisions, computers, and video recorders. They attract the eye even when they are not switched on. Furniture stores now stock antique reproduction cabinets to conceal high-tech appliances, but they do tend to be expensive and look cheap. If you watch a lot of television it isn't practical to hide it in a cupboard, but you could take it off its stand and put it on something more in keeping with the room's style, such as a tin trunk or a wooden chest. If the room has an alcove, push the equipment back into it, and fit a wide shelf at least 12 in. above it. A blind or curtain can be fitted along the shelf edge to conceal everything when not in use. A folding screen is an even easier solution, and it also offers more decorative possibilities.

HOW TO DO IT

STEP 1 Apply wood glue to the joining edges and assemble the frames. Screw to fasten. Paint the frames and the molding with a primer, an undercoat, and the final top coat.

STEP 2 Lay the frame over the fabric and cut, leaving at least 1½ in. as an overlap.

STEP 3 Stretch the fabric tight and staple it to the back of the frame. Place the first four staples halfway along each side, then staple the corners and several points in between.

STEP 4 Measure the lengths of braid needed to cover the edges. Miter the corners, then apply fabric adhesive to the back edges.

STEP 5 Lay the three screen panels flat, butted up together, and place hinges 4 in. from the top and bottom, with one in the middle. Use the bradawl to make small pilot holes for the screws.

STEP 6 Small round feet can be added using brass or wooden cupboard door knobs screwed into the base of the frames.

A folding screen is a portable and decorative way of hiding modern equipment such as computers, televisions, and video recorders.

VARIATIONS
• Fit the sheets of woven cane in the same way as the fabric.
• Use small screws to secure the fretwork panels to the frames. You will need to drill clearance holes along the panel edges, and use a bradawl to make pilot holes for the screws. Paint the panels to match or contrast with the frames.

Contemporary sitting room

The really big influences over the past few years have been minimalism, modern art, and eco-awareness. And a more open-plan style for living has filtered down from Manhattan lofts, while the rediscovery of 1960s high-rise apartments has found its way into everyday decorating. It is also true to say that we may not all aspire to live in converted warehouses, but we can still appreciate the clarity of an uncluttered space furnished with a few interesting pieces.

We can even try glass bricks that let light filter through to create an airy feel. In fact, comfort areas are more clearly defined than ever, with sheepskin rugs on hard floors, huge sofas, low tables, and lighting directed toward the seating and decorative objects. The trick is to keep colors muted and natural for a really airy feel, and introduce them by masking off and painting blocks of color to break up the wall space. You should also add some contemporary art. This can be anything from an abstract painting to a large rock, a weather-beaten tree trunk, or a large desert cactus. Just do it with confidence! Fifteen sure ways to give your sitting room a contemporary style are…

Muted, natural colors help the contemporary style by giving an airy feel. Soft throws folded over the backs of sofas add to the style.

Floating wooden floor

The new wooden floor looks different to stripped pine floorboards, the wood strips are narrower and the boards are butted up, leaving no gaps. The design principle is the same for most brands of strip flooring, although quality and price vary quite a lot. Tongue-and-groove boards are laminated with a veneer of real lumber and are laid on top of existing level flooring. This sort of flooring has the look and feel of wood, but is laid with the convenience of vinyl.

Glass shelving and wooden storage cubes

Glass is a strong, natural material and an essential ingredient in contemporary style. An alcove fitted with toughened glass shelves looks superb and can be used to display anything from a row of pebbles to a collection of magazines, but you will need to consider fitting concealed lighting as well. It's only when glass and light are combined that the full effect becomes clear. Use frosted glass or glass bricks as screening between rooms to create a barrier without losing the sense of space.

Eco-friendly materials

Caring about the environment means being picky about the materials with which you decorate your home. So many chemicals infect

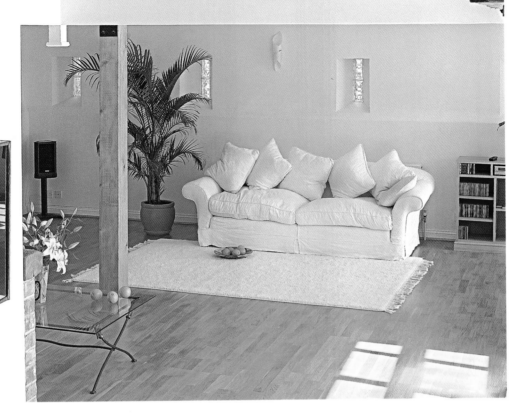

Wooden floors are a must in any contemporary sitting room, but new, floating wooden floors make it easier than ever before to create this look.

the air of the home these days, all in the name of treating mold, stains, bacteria, and good old wear and tear. If you want a more natural environment, there are organic and eco-friendly paint ranges, carpets, fabrics, and cleaning materials. They will do you no harm, and may prevent allergies as well.

Rugs and fabrics

Hard wooden floors give a fabulous look, but they need to be comfortable, too, especially when walking barefoot. Rugs have made a comeback recently, and all fashionable furniture outlets have ranges of colorful or neutral designer rugs, ethnic kilims, natural matting, and soft sheepskins. Rugs can be used to define a seating or eating area in an open-plan room. Spend as much as you can on them and make a real feature of them by putting them on show —don't waste them under chairs and sofas! Felt, wool, mohair, and rough-weave cotton are the key fabrics to use.

Blinds or sheer curtains

Contemporary window dressing has no time for flounces and frills. Fit wooden Venetian or handmade paper blinds, or hang plain, tab-topped curtains from a pole. King-size, white, Egyptian cotton sheets look stunning clipped onto a rail, or if you need to inject some spicy colors, drape exquisitely embroidered sari fabrics, or hand-blocked Japanese textiles from a curtain pole. Vintage patterned fabrics and brocades combined with plain bands of color are also very chic and stylish.

Low coffee table

A long, low coffee table looks great, providing it is not piled up with clutter. Favorite styles also include designs with storage space beneath the table top. Chrome or aluminum legs with 1970s-style rosewood laminates, tubular chrome and glass, pale wood with industrial-size casters, and roughly-hewn, African dark wood versions are all considered to be extremely cool.

If you have the space, over-size, dramatic houseplants like this one will add an organic feel to your contemporary sitting room, without making it seem cluttered.

Leather cushions, armchair, or cube

Classic leather and chrome chairs, such as the Barcelona and Wassily chairs, were designed in the first half of the last century and, although they have been copied, they have never been bettered. If your finances don't stretch to a designer chair, then a leather cube, or even a cushion will show that you're on the right track.

Lamps and candles

Table lamps need to be quite large—think of large, organic-shape ceramic or wooden table lamps with plain, cream shades, or tall and simple metal standard lamps. High-tech, tracked spotlighting systems are also fine for illuminating CD collections or books. Large multi-wick candles, or tealights in a row of matching glasses are also good for creating an atmosphere.

Large, plain-colored sofa

Big, plain-colored sofas are very much part of the contemporary-style sitting room. The most stylish sofas have a boxy shape, with ultra-generous seating and short legs. These sofas are made for putting your feet up and relaxing. Comfort is the essential antidote to all this fashionable minimalism.

Soft, folded, pashmina-style throws

The other concession to comfort comes from being able to drape your furniture and yourself in beautiful, soft, woolen throws. Fold them over the arms of chairs or the back of the sofa and use them as comforters on cool nights. Pashmina shawls are the best, but anything from a fringed cot blanket, or a mohair stole, to a plaid travel rug will work if the colors are right.

Decluttering

This word may not be in the dictionary, but we all know what it means. It used to be called being neat, or putting things away, but now we call it "decluttering." There are even stores, catalogs, consultants, and entire books dedicated to the art. If you have a great deal of money, you can even hire someone for $300 an hour to come round and tell you to throw out most of your stuff and put the rest of it in labeled boxes. If you would prefer a few homemade ideas, then read on …

CDs

Free up space currently used to hold your CD collection by buying a wall-mounted CD storage unit. Make sure you buy one with more space than you need. Allow for at least a third more slots than the CDs you currently own, and edit the collection as new CDs are added.

Magazines

An acrylic or bent beechwood magazine rack will look perfect, and keep magazines and color supplements neat and tidy. Keep only the current editions in your rack, and store back issues on a bookshelf in magazine box files.

Video tapes

Video tape covers are competitively garish on purpose so that they stand out from the thousands of other videos in the store. But they never look good at home, so put them away! Choose an easily accessible storage system suitable for the number of tapes you own. Woven baskets, or heavy board boxes with lids are a good idea. If you own a lot of tapes, make long, plain MDF boxes with hinged flaps that can be fitted onto the wall. Use a beech or maple-veneered MDF for the front, or paint it the same color as the walls.

Storage space down below

Choose a low table with compartments or drawers, and stand lamps on cubes or drums that can also be used to hide clutter—this only works if you go through it regularly and sort things out!

Fitted shelving units with doors and drawers

If there is one good lesson to be learned from minimalism, it is that not everything is worth displaying. Choose a few decorative objects for open, glass shelves, and keep the rest behind closed doors.

The contemporary sitting room is clutter-free, which requires a little day-to-day discipline of putting things away behind closed doors.

THE PROJECTS

The projects on the following pages will help achieve the basic elements of any contemporary sitting room: the wooden floor and the coffee table. Some disciplined decluttering, a large, plain-colored sofa, and a big rug will do the rest.

Laying a floating wooden floor

Laminated flooring is a fashion that's here to stay. It's easy to lay, looks a million dollars, and is really easy to keep clean. It's made in average floorboard width and comes in a wide range of stained hardwood veneers, varying between $3/8$ in. and $3/4$ in. in depth. The best are the most expensive—surprise, surprise. Laminates are stain resistant, won't splinter, and because of their tongue-and-groove fitting, you avoid drafts coming up through gaps in the floorboards.

Existing floors need to be levelled before you begin. Concrete floors will need a heavy-duty PVC damp-proof membrane, and all floors need a good underlay of either $5/16$-in. felt boards or $1/8$-in. foam sheeting. When you buy laminated flooring, you will also need a fitting kit and laminated flooring adhesive. The kit will contain full fitting instructions and spacers to be inserted between the floor and the skirting board, because the floor will expand after it has been laid.

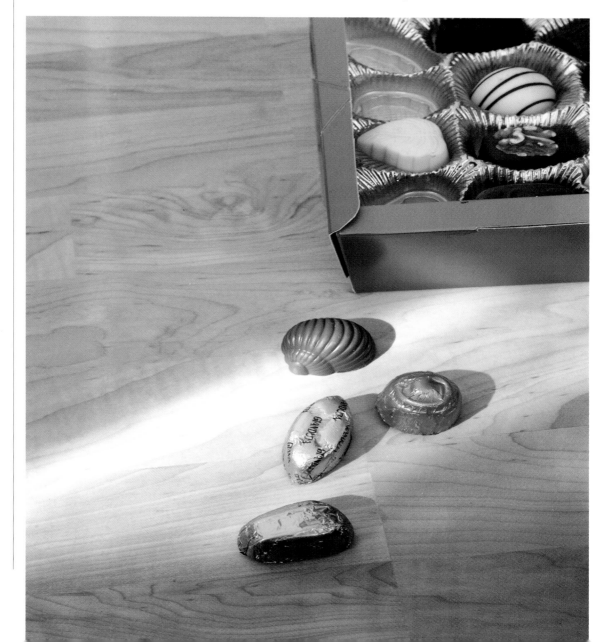

Laminated flooring is stain-resistant, splinter-, and draft-free. It comes in a range of stained veneers, the best of which are the most expensive.

HOW TO DO IT

STEP 1 Put down the underlay, butting the joints together.

STEP 2 Lay the first board with the groove on the edge next to the wall. Place spacers at the end and along the wall.

STEP 3 Lay another board loosely (without glue) at the end of the first, engaging the tongue and groove. Add another board or, depending upon the space, cut one to fit the remaining space, allowing enough room for a spacer next to the wall. Use a string line to check that the boards are straight, otherwise the other boards will be out of line as well.

STEP 4 Run a continuous line of adhesive along the tongue and groove.

STEP 5 Use the tamping block with a hammer to force the boards tightly together.

STEP 6 Immediately wipe off the excess glue, which will ooze out between the joints, with a damp cloth. Begin the second row with the off-cut from the first, providing it is at least 12 in. long. Lay the first three rows, and leave the adhesive to dry before you continue. The last row of boards may have to be cut across its width to fit into the space, and you must remember to allow for the spacers. Finally, remove the spacers and fit the quarter-round molding to the skirting to cover the expansion gap.

YOU WILL NEED:

• 4 LENGTHS OF
  PREPARED LUMBER;
  16 x 1 ³/₄ IN.
• 4 BATTENS; 2 x ⁷/₈ IN.
• 2 SCRAPS OF SHOEBOX
  CARDBOARD
• WOOD GLUE
• 8 x 2-IN. No. 6
  SCREWS
• ¹/₈-IN. DRILL BIT
• DRILL
• DARK WOODSTAIN
• BRUSH
• TAPE MEASURE
• COMBINATION
  SQUARE
• PENCIL
• SCREWDRIVER
• WAX POLISH
  AND CLOTH

PROJECT TWO

Making a coffee table

The best coffee tables are long, low, and simply elegant, the focus being on a good shape and finish. This one is made from four main pieces of prepared lumber, with hidden battens to support the legs. Construction could not be more simple, and the wood can be stained deep tan or dark brown to suit the contemporary room style that has been chosen.

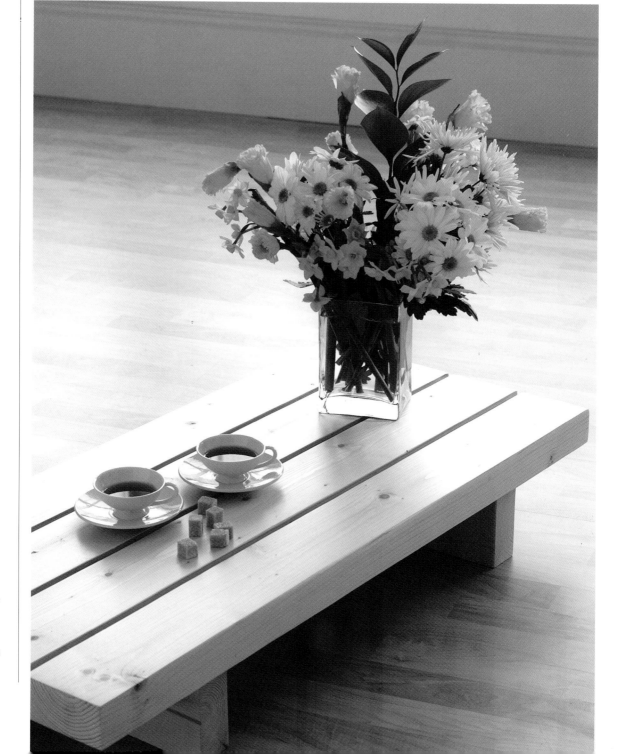

This long, low, and elegant coffee table is easy to construct from just four main pieces of prepared lumber, with hidden batons to support the legs.

HOW TO DO IT

STEP 1 Butt together the four long planks of wood on a flat work surface, and lace the three scraps between them to make narrow gaps. Mark 12 in. from each end and use the combination square and a pencil to draw a line across both planks.

STEP 2 Lay out the four lengths of batten and draw in the halfway line (3 in.). Drill a hole in the middle of each half on all four pieces. Place one batten along the inside of each of the lines across the two planks. Coat the battens with wood glue and then screw them to the planks.

STEP 3 Draw a center guideline across the width of each leg.

STEP 4 Apply a liberal coating of wood glue to the base of each of the legs and to the side of the batten then, having lined them up with the gap, put both legs in place.

STEP 5 Now fix a second batten to the other side of the leg to hold it firmly from both sides. Apply wood glue to the surfaces and screw the battens to the planks. Leave to bond overnight. (This is very important, no matter what it says on the tube!)

STEP 6 Apply a coat or two of woodstain, tinted varnish, or wax polish.

Global sitting room

This is a room where color leads and everything else follows on. If you love color, then this is the way to proceed, and it's a very helpful approach if you are starting from scratch and don't know where to begin. Once you have decided on, say, burnt orange, pale blue, and cream for the walls, then the furniture and accessories can be chosen because they look great against that background.

(Right) This Moroccan-style room displays the elaborately carved furniture and exotic colors traditional to the region.

A color scheme can be inspired by anything that you see about you, from a bowl of fresh fruit or flowers to your favorite candy wrapper or the background in a vacation photo. In fact, it is easier to find paint to match a color that you have already chosen than it is to begin by staring at a paint chart for inspiration. Charts are fantastic once you know what you're looking for, but confusing when you don't.

Color ranges get bigger, brighter, and bolder all the time, and whereas a few years ago you could only buy strong colors for walls from an expensive paint specializer, they now appear in the hardware stores' own ranges at a fraction of the price. Test pots allow you to experiment with colors and are far more helpful than a small rectangle on a white background. And if you only want a small amount for an area of intense color, they do the job at a great price.

Tricks with color

There is no doubt that the TV decorating programs have had a massive influence on the way we think about using color at home. Most rules regarding good taste have been broken in the quest for more riveting TV, and this has actually been quite liberating. Now it's OK to say that you chose turquoise and lime with a splash of silver-leaf gilding because it took your fancy!

Also note that blocks of color can be used to create dramatic effects in a room. As a rule, red foreshortens a room, bringing the walls in closer, while blue recedes. This is the way our eyes read these colors, and you can use them to stretch or compact a space accordingly. Play visual tricks with color. For example, yellow lightens and brightens rooms, and is really useful when a room doesn't get much natural daylight. Color also affects our moods, making us feel happy, tranquil, excited, or irritable, which is something to bear in mind when you are doing up your global sitting room.

THE PROJECTS

Color ranges have associations with different cultures and climates. This means that you can conjure up the mood of another place using its characteristic colors. The following three projects show how you can use color to create an African, Moroccan, or Mediterranean style. A low divan bed, rough-textured wall, and a small table are the common starting points.

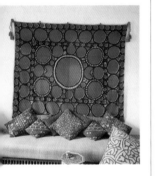

Deep, earthy reds in a symmetrical pattern conjure up the heat of North Africa.

Cool stone floors, earthy colored textiles in bold patterns, and an open fire bring a taste of Africa to this sitting room.

PROJECT ONE

The African room

The colors of Africa are drawn from the landscape: rusty reds and dark, mud browns of the earth, yellow ochers of the sun, and pale, sky blues are combined with the rich, ebony black of cooking pots on the open fire. The style is plain, with organic shapes and bold patterns. Look out for woven and printed African textiles for throws and cushion covers, wood-carved figures, woven grass matting, clay pots, gourd bowls, and recycled African tin and wirework.

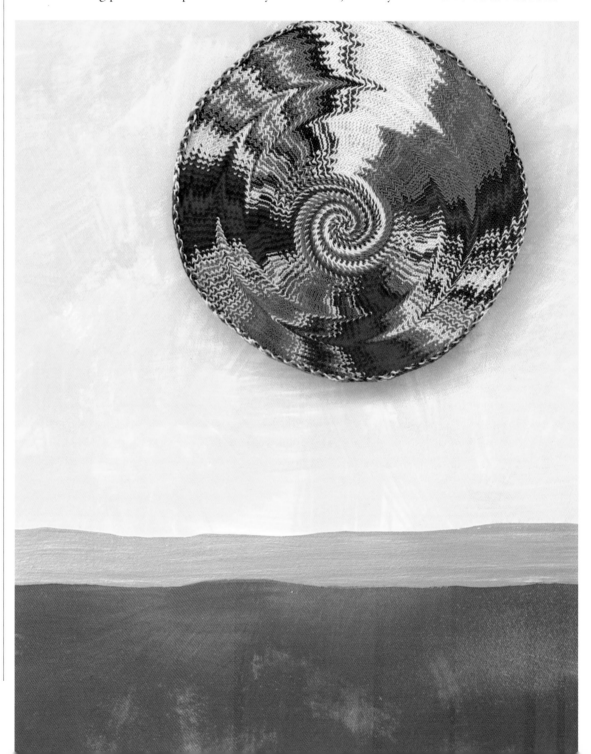

This African-style wall reflects the colors of the landscape—the rusty red of the earth, the soft, yellow ocher of the sun, and the blue sky between. A woven grass mat in a bold, spiral pattern completes the effect.

HOW TO DO IT

STEP 1 Stain the floorboards using a very dark woodstain. Measure and mark 39 in. up the wall from the floor and stick up a line of painter's tape.

STEP 2 Paint the wall above the tape a soft, yellow ocher color. Use random brush strokes to sweep the color in different directions.

STEP 3 Paint from the floor to the tape in a rich, earthy red.

STEP 4 Remove the tape and paint a freehand brush line using a pale stone-colored paint. Don't be nervous— it should look hand-painted.

STEP 5 Cover the divan with a rough-weave African cloth, tucked under tightly at the edges. Add cushions covered in dark brown and cream, or indigo blue, batik-patterned cottons, or fabric patterned like zebra, giraffe, or leopard skin.

STEP 6 Use grass matting on the floor, baskets woven from grasses, gourd bowls, a pendant light with an African sun hat as a shade, a small table painted black, and a top covered with a woven place mat.

PROJECT TWO
The Moroccan room

The north of Africa has an Arab culture where strong Islamic principles influence the decorative traditions. The homes have cool marble floors, arched shuttered windows, and mathematical patterns everywhere. The look is exotic, mysterious, and highly stylized. Look out for tasselled and mirrored textiles, kilim rugs, small, carved shelves, and Ali Baba pots.

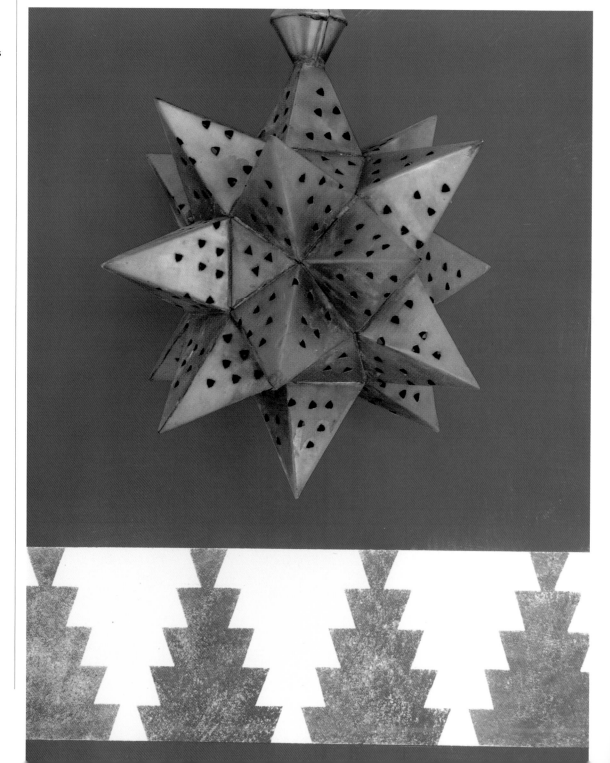

This stepped, geometric pattern border stencilled along the skirting board shows the mathematical patterns typical of the Moroccan decorative tradition. Moroccan rugs, tasselled cushions, and an arched, framed mirror add to the look.

HOW TO DO IT

STEP 1 Mark a tile's depth white border at baseboard level.

STEP 2 Paint the wall above the border in a deep blue paint.

STEP 3 Stencil the stepped geometric pattern border along the baseboard (stencil pattern provided) in emerald green, deep red, and black on white.

STEP 4 Lay Moroccan rugs and durries overlapping each other to cover the floor. Hang an arched framed mirror, beaded bags, mirrored cloth wall hangings, and small carved shelves on the wall.

STEP 5 Place a date palm in an Ali Baba pot on the floor, and a large brass tray on the small table, laid with a set of Moroccan tea glasses.

YOU WILL NEED:
- PAINT
- CHAIR RAIL
- PANEL ADHESIVE
- COUNTERSUNK
  SCREWS
- STENCIL PAPER
- SCALPEL
- BRUSH
- ACCESSORIES SUCH
  AS GERANIUMS IN
  TERRACOTTA POTS,
  BRASS OIL LAMPS,
  BLUE AND WHITE
  CUSHIONS,
  PATTERNED PLATES,
  AND SMALL PICTURES
  IN FRAMES

PROJECT THREE

The Mediterranean room

There are many countries and islands around the Mediterranean Sea, and each has its own distinctive decorating style. The influence of the warm, dry climate is seen in the cool interiors with tiled floors and shuttered windows. White is the dominant color, its brilliance enhanced by the azure blue sky. The dry climate simplifies the decorating, because no sealants are needed. Walls are painted with chalky distemper and wood is left unvarnished. There are different traditional embroidery, weaving, ceramic, and ironwork patterns throughout the Mediterranean.

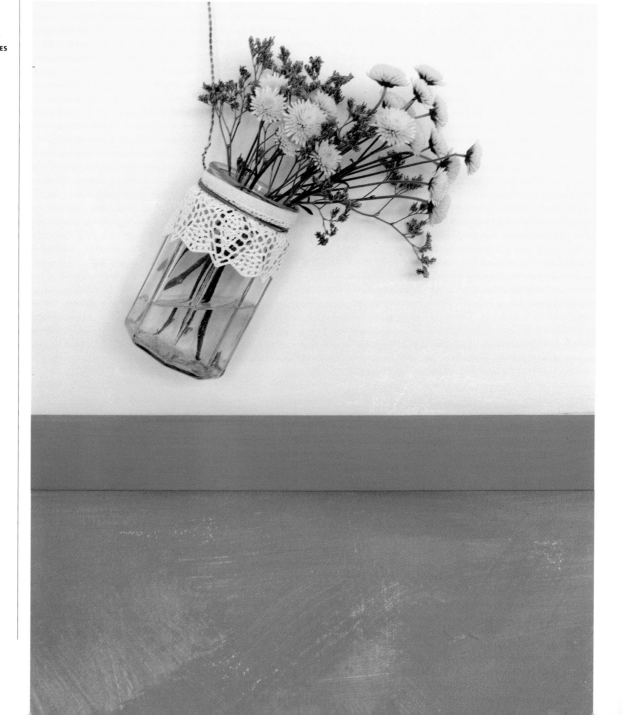

This wall has been divided using a wooden molding painted a deep turquoise blue. The paint above and below has a chalky texture. A group of small pictures in frames, and a grapevine stencil painted along the top of the wall complete the effect.

HOW TO DO IT

STEP 1 Divide the wall at the height that a chair rail would be, using a wooden molding. This can be applied with panel adhesive and strengthened with a few countersunk screws.

STEP 2 Paint the lower half of the wall with a plaster pink, chalky finish paint.

STEP 3 Paint the top half using a chalky-textured cream paint.

STEP 4 Paint the chair rail deep turquoise or cobalt blue.

STEP 5 Stencil a grapevine along the top of the wall. This does not have to look realistic in vine colors, just stencil it in one color to look like a shadow in dark green or terracotta.

STEP 6 Cover the divan with a blue and white Greek embroidered bedspread, and hang up a Greek fisherman's lamp.

STEP 7 Hang a rustic, unvarnished, wooden shelf and a group of small pictures in frames. Cover the table with a white lace-edged cloth and a vase of bright flowers. Add red geraniums in terracotta pots, blue and white rustic ceramic wares, and a rush-seated chair.

Enlarge the stencil below and transfer the pattern to plastic or stencil paper. Cut out carefully using a sharp snap-blade knife.

Tiny sitting room

With a small room, you have to decide whether to accept it and decorate without deception, or to play tricks with color, light, and mirrors to create an illusion of a bigger space. Many apartment conversions have left rooms that are either tall and narrow, or low and long, but it's amazing what a few tricks of color, furnishing, and lighting will do to change the apparent shape of the room. Whatever you choose, you will have to maximize all the space you have by organizing your possessions and using every storage trick in the book, from disguised drawers to making the most of any nooks and crannies.

The first thing you need to think about is how many people will regularly use the sitting room. If it will be no more than two, then a small sofa and a place for the television, stereo, and coffee table are all that's really needed. If it's more than two, you need to get creative!

Small is beautiful

If you decide to make a feature of the room's diminutive size, it can be made into a very sexy, tactile space where the edges between furniture, floor, and walls are blurred. Remember the shagpile carpet. It must be due for a revival and wouldn't break the bank in a tiny room; an alternative option would be a long-haired rug like the flokati, another 1970s favorite, which is handwoven with a very thick, shaggy, wool pile. A low couch, felt cushions, knitted throws, and fake fur rugs are other things to consider. A sheepskin-covered bean bag would be the ultimate accessory. The lower walls can either be covered with a soft-textured wallpaper, or even be lined with fabric like a Bedouin tent. Emphasize the coziness by painting the room a dark color, such as deep red or chocolate brown, with gilded woodwork, and have plenty of warm, low lighting and thick curtains. Vintage velvets, draped felt, or dyed blankets buttoned over a pole all work well.

Think big

If you decide that the challenge is to make everyone believe that the room is twice its actual size, then your first accessory has to be a mirror. If an entire wall is lined with mirror tiles the room will appear double its size, but there are more subtle ways of using mirrors that will make the space appear bigger, and make the shape look more interesting as well. You will need to watch the lighting, however because the reflections can be blinding. A pair of wooden window frames fitted with mirrors will give the appearance of looking into another room, long mirrors placed across the corners of the room will make it look octagonal, and a large, arched, framed mirror will appear to be a doorway into an adjoining room. Plants in front of mirrors will also look twice as bushy, thanks to the reflection. Use pale colors, playing around with two or three different tones of yellow, light blue, or green. The deeper shades will appear to recede and give shape to flat walls.

Doors and windows

Windows are best played down by fitting blinds or shutters into the frame. Keep the color the same or lighter than that of the walls. A half-glazed door or a window onto a passageway is a means of including the space outside the room.

You can make a feature out of a small room like this one by deciding firmly what it will be used for before you start. This one is definitely a reading room. A long, low couch in neutral colors blends into the surrounding walls. Floor-to-ceiling bookcases complete the look.

And if you could do without the door altogether, it could be removed to give a more open-plan feel to the room.

Tall rooms

In old buildings that have been converted into apartments, the ceilings are often very high. This is fabulous when the room is in proportion, but all too often large reception rooms have been sectioned off and the resulting rooms are narrow and tall. There are a few simple tricks that will help to squash the room into shape. Paint the ceiling and cornice down to picture-rail height using a dark, flat color. Hang the lights so that they emerge below this level and cast the light downward. Use a patterned carpet or rugs to attract the eye downward, and hang pictures a bit lower than you normally would. If you would prefer to do something more substantial, why not build a

platform to raise one half of the room up to a different level? This would create useful storage space at the same time.

Short rooms

If your tiny room has a low ceiling and you need to raise the roof, then similar tricks can be used in reverse. Vertical stripes have an elongating effect, and a white ceiling with no center light will give the room a lift. Use spotlights to pick out pictures or interesting objects, and wall uplighters for ambient light.

THE PROJECTS
The projects on the following pages show two ways of making the most of a small room. The first uses an aluminum-leaf wall to make a room look bigger, and the second shows how to make a drawer disguised as part of the baseboard.

YOU WILL NEED:

- SILVER FLAT LATEX PAINT, WHICH MUST BE WATER-BASED
- ALUMINUM LEAF (SOLD IN ART STORES, GENERALLY IN PACKS OF 25 SQUARE LEAVES)
- WATER-BASED GOLD SIZE (GLUE)
- ENAMEL OR SEMIGLOSS VARNISH
- ROLLER AND TRAY
- PAINT BRUSH
- SOFT CLOTH
- LONG RULE

PROJECT ONE

Covering a wall with foil squares

A surface that reflects light will blur the boundaries as well. This project shows how to use squares of aluminum leaf to create a glowing wall in a small room. If you like the idea but would find a whole wall overpowering, why not begin by lining an alcove? Silver looks good with pale wood, frosted glass, and smart, navy blue furniture.

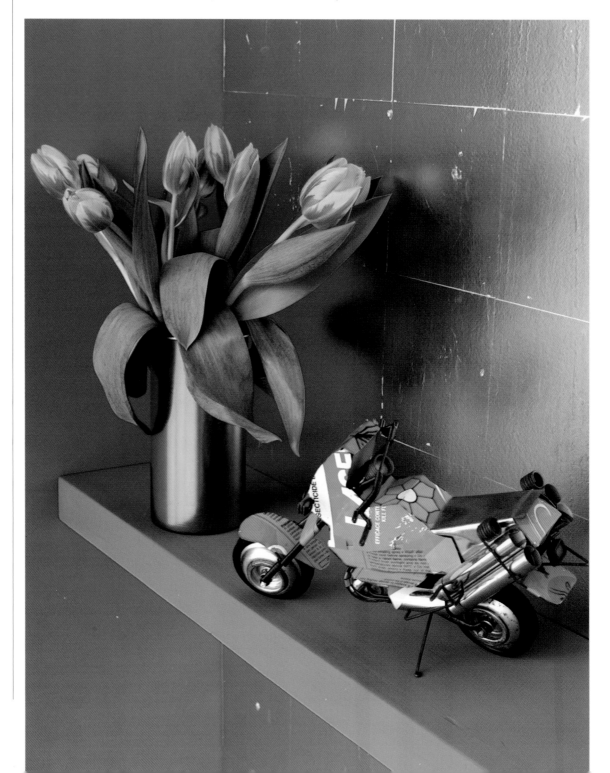

An aluminum-leaf wall reflects the colors around it, blending into the walls on either side.

HOW TO DO IT

STEP 1 Apply two coats of silver paint to the wall, allowing the correct drying times before and after the second coat.

STEP 2 Measure out a section of wall big enough for nine squares, and apply the glue. Leave it for about 15 minutes until it feels tacky. Begin applying the leaf in one of the top corners, pressing the square gently onto the wall and rubbing the back lightly with your fingers.

STEP 3 Slowly peel the backing paper off from top to bottom. If any of the leaf remains on the paper, replace it, and rub the back again lightly. Line the next square up to the edge of the first. Continue in the same way, fitting the squares in sections until the wall is covered.

STEP 4 Buff the leaf to a gleaming shine using a lint-free soft cloth. Apply a coat of semigloss or enamel varnish to protect your work of art.

YOU WILL NEED:
- 8 SMALL CASTERS
- LENGTH OF BASEBOARD TO MATCH THE EXISTING ONE (IF IT CAN'T BE RE-USED)
- PANEL ADHESIVE
- 2 x 1 IN. BATTEN
- ½-IN. MDF SHEET FOR SHELF
- ¼-IN. MDF FOR DRAWER BASE
- ¼-IN. MDF FOR 4 DRAWER SIDES
- BACKSAW
- THIN BRADS
- SMALL HAMMER
- PAINT AND BRUSH
- SPIRIT LEVEL
- DRILL
- MASONRY BIT
- WALL ANCHORS

PROJECT TWO

Disguised storage

If you really want to disguise something, the trick is to make it look the same as everything around it. This project does this by building a boxed-in shelf with a drawer at floor level, and using a baseboard front to disguise it so well that it could almost be used as a safe. This is also a way to make the most of an alcove by building the shelf wide enough for the TV. If the alcove is not deep enough, it will need to be built out at the front, but the basic idea remains the same.

This drawer on casters has been built as part of a low, boxed-in shelf, and disguised with a baseboard front to blend in with the edges around it.

HOW TO DO IT

STEP 1 Measure the depth of the alcove. If it needs extending, take this into account and cut out 2 side pieces of 2 x 1 in. to support the shelf. If the shelf height is 19 ³/₄ in., the sides will need to be 19 ¹/₄ in. Drill and screw to the wall, and then check the level.

STEP 2 Cut the shelf to fit the alcove. Cut a U-shape cable hole on the back edge. Apply a long bead of adhesive to the top edges of the sides and place the shelf on top. Use a hammer to drive in some thin brads to hold the shelf securely. If the alcove is wide, add a supporting leg to the middle.

STEP 3 Make up the two drawers: cut the base of each drawer to fit snugly inside the alcove, allowing just enough clearance for it to slide in and out without catching.

STEP 4 Cut drawer sides to match the depth of the shelf, and a front and back to be butted into them.

STEP 5 Fit four casters to the base of each drawer.

STEP 6 Cut the baseboard to fit onto the drawer front (and box sides if the shelf has been built out beyond the alcove). Stick the baseboard onto the drawer front (and box sides if built out) with panel adhesive. Do this so that the baseboard skims the floor, hiding the casters. Paint the sides and front of the drawers to match the walls and the front to match the baseboard.

Dining rooms

Good food, good wine, and good company are made even more special by a stylish dining room, but even the simplest of meals can be made into a special occasion by a beautiful setting. Because the dining room is all about eating, much of the style is down to the table and chairs, but flooring, lighting, and color can have just the same impact. This section shows you how to transform your dining room into one of three different styles: Traditional, Contemporary, or Sitting-dining room. The step-by-step projects will start you off, and a fresh coat of paint and some flexible lighting should do the rest.

Traditional dining room

The dining room is the place to indulge yourself. There was a time when most family life took place here—meals were eaten around the table, and that was also where children played and did their homework. Fashions change, however, and after the 1960s homes were built with dining areas rather than whole dining rooms. In older houses internal walls were knocked down to make kitchens bigger, and after that walls were knocked down between living rooms and dining rooms as well, to make even larger open-plan spaces. Dining rooms became something of a luxury, because only people with large houses still had them.

Wooden chairs with upholstered seats can be revamped with a fresh coat of paint and a change of fabric.

It has taken a while, but with the top two leisure activities now being cooking and decorating, there has been a natural progression toward reinstating the dining room. It is now thought extremely stylish to invite your guests into your dining room to serve them a lovely meal, without a television or kitchen sink in sight. Traditional dining rooms also make it a lot easier to cheat with the cooking when the chef is out of sight next door.

Chairs

The key ingredients in a classy dining room are the chairs. You can always fake the table by using an elegant tablecloth to cover an old door on saw horses, but the chairs will be on show and should be as good looking and as comfortable as they possibly can be.

The great thing about opting for the traditional style is that you can always pick up secondhand dining room chairs for a reasonable price in flea markets or at an auction. The trick is to buy them one, two, or three at a time, because they are always much cheaper than in sets of four or more. They don't even have to match, so long as they are of more or less the same period and style. In fact, a slightly mismatched collection of

chairs can look really chic if you decorate them in the same way.

The Swedish Gustavian style is well suited to this treatment, and it is a classic look that manages to appear traditional and fresh at the same time. Paint the woodwork matte white and give it a "mildly distressed" look by rubbing the paint back to the bare wood in places with sandpaper. The seats can be covered with a red, yellow, or blue gingham or stripe.

Wooden chairs with upholstered seats can easily be given a whole new style with a change of fabric and a lick of paint. Strip the wood of its old varnish and re-stain it a deep, rich brown, and then cover the seats with a warm-colored velvet or brocade fabric. Look out for remnants of good quality upholstery fabric, or even old curtains which are often abandoned when people move house and find their new homes have different-shape windows.

Tables

Tables are usually expensive and are one of the few pieces of furniture that seem to hold their value, whether they are in fashion or not. Choose a table with the right proportions for your room—there must be enough space for you to

A chandelier over the dining table is the centerpiece to the traditional dining room. Traditional-style, matching cutlery, linen napkins, and fresh flowers add the finishing touch.

move around it, pull out the chairs, and serve a meal without having to hug the wall. Most traditional dining tables have hidden fold-out flaps so that they can expand from four or six to eight or ten settings. They are ideal for occasional entertaining. The only other furniture needed in a dining room is a console table, sideboard, or trolley for the food.

Colors

Colors can be rich, strong, and dramatic in dining rooms. Hang large-frame pictures and mirrors on the walls, and go to town with the curtains and lighting as well. If you own a chandelier, then this is the place to use it. Candlelight turns a meal into an occasion, and a candelabra hung over the table will bring an air of grandeur to even the simplest of meals. Keep a look out for an old chandelier in a flea market—it will often need mending and rewiring, but it will be worth it.

If the room is warm enough to do without a carpet, then why not try stencilling a border pattern on the floor? This is a good way to get the unifying look of an expensive carpet at a fraction of the price. There are some fabulous stencil patterns on the market, and with a few cans of stencil paint and a dash of confidence, you could paint anything from a simple, folk-art border to a very convincing Turkish carpet in your spare time. And don't forget the finishing touches—a smooth white tablecloth with matching napkins, traditional-style cutlery, sparkling glassware, and a vase of fresh flowers.

THE PROJECTS

The two projects on the following pages show how to paint broad, vertical stripes in the traditional style, and how to revamp old dining chairs in the Gustavian (Swedish) style, complete with new, matching upholstery.

PROJECT ONE

Painting broad stripes with a roller

There is no need to be restrained just because you have decided to decorate the dining room in a traditional style. If you are doing French Empire style, the stripes can be broad, bold, black, and gold; if your theme is Swedish, make them yellow and grey. Arts and Crafts colors are earthy, woody green, and rust red. Every traditional style has certain key patterns and colors, and these stripes are a quick and easy way to give your room a dramatic new look.

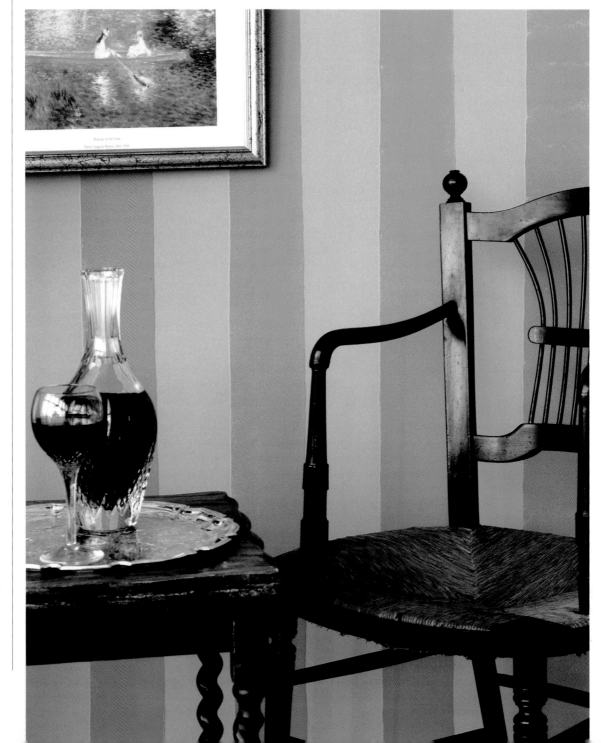

Broad, vertical stripes painted in colors to suit a particular traditional style are an easy way to give your dining room a completely new look.

HOW TO DO IT

STEP 1 Decide whether you want the stripes to go the full length of the wall, or just up to the picture rail. Here, we are painting a horizontal stripe at picture-rail height. Room heights vary, so judge this by eye. Hang the plumb line above the height of the stripe, and use the rule to mark the stripe's position along the wall.

STEP 2 Follow the marks with a line of painter's tape between the corners. Paint the lighter background color between the baseboard and the tape, and leave to dry.

STEP 3 Put the second color in the small roller tray and mix it half and half with pre-mixed wallpaper paste. Run the roller through the paint until evenly coated.

STEP 4 Make a stripe guide by marking the painter's tape with the roller, leaving a roller's width between the stripes.

STEP 5 With the plumb line as a guide, run the roller down the wall in a straight line. Do not press too hard, but keep the pressure even. Stop just short of the baseboard and re-charge the roller. Continue in this way, moving the plumb line as you progress, so that you don't drift off the vertical.

STEP 6 When the wall is finished, dip the small sponge into the paint and use it to stamp the rest of the line up to the baseboard (the roller will not reach this last bit).

STEP 7 Remove the painter's tape and leave the paint to dry. Now run a line of painter's tape with its top edge along the top of the stripes, and then another 2 in. above it. Check it with the spirit level.

STEP 8 Use the brush to paint inside the painter's tape using the striping color, or a contrasting color to match the baseboard if you prefer. Peel away the tape when the paint has dried.

YOU WILL NEED:

- CHAIR WITH
  A PADDED
  DROP-IN SEAT
- PAINT AND VARNISH
  STRIPPER
- PAINT BRUSH
- NEWSPAPER
- RUBBER GLOVES
- SCRAPER
- STEEL WOOL
- MINERAL SPIRITS
- FLAT WHITE PAINT
- CANDLE
- PAINT BRUSH OR
  SMALL FOAM ROLLER
  AND TRAY
- SANDPAPER

PROJECT TWO

Doing up a dining chair

Everyday furniture used to be far better made than it is now, so it really makes sense to buy a selection of old dining chairs with drop-in or upholstered seats. These are not expensive antiques, but chairs from the days when every home had a dining room table and chairs. A tall-back design is best for this Gustavian (Swedish) style, and it is amazing how much of a set an odd bunch will look once they have been given a similar paint finish and upholstery.

Old dining chairs can be transformed into this Gustavian style using a distressed paint finish and reupholstering in red, yellow, or blue gingham, or stripes.

HOW TO DO THE PAINTING

STEP 1 Put on the rubber gloves and stand the chair on newspaper. Cover it in a thick coating of paint stripper and wait for the surface to bubble up.

STEP 2 Scrape off the paint or varnish, taking care to drop all the waste onto the newspaper.

STEP 3 Dip the steel wool in mineral spirits and clean off the remaining paint or varnish. Leave to dry.

STEP 4 Rub the edges of the chair and any raised pattern on the wood, the curve of the legs and the seat corners with the candle. A light stroke will be enough.

STEP 5 Apply two coats of the white paint, allowing the correct drying time between and after.

STEP 6 Rub the waxed areas with sandpaper. The paint should lift away easily, so that the bare wood shows through in places. It is important not to overdo this effect, because it is meant to simulate natural wear and tear.

YOU WILL NEED:

- TACK LIFTER
- CALICO
- CHECKED FABRIC
- STAPLE GUN OR TACKS
  AND A SMALL
  UPHOLSTERY
  HAMMER
- BRAID FOR EDGING
  (OPTIONAL)
- FABRIC GLUE
- PINS

HOW TO DO THE UPHOLSTERY

STEP 1 Strip off the old fabric and remove the old tacks and staples. Replace the seat pad if necessary.

STEP 2 Lay the calico over the seat and cut it to fit, allowing enough to fold down the sides and turn over a small hem.

STEP 3 Use the calico as a template and cut out the checked fabric, adding an extra ¾ in. on all sides so that it will overlap the calico on the seat. Turn over and press a small hem on both pieces.

STEP 4 Lay the calico over the seat and fix it to the frame in the middle of one side first, then stretch it across and staple it in the middle of the opposite side. Do the same with the back and front.

STEP 5 Fold a triangle under at each corner and staple this flat to the frame on both sides. Do this on opposite corners, and then pleat the excess fabric over and staple it to the frame. Fix the calico all the way around the seat.

STEP 6 Fix the checked fabric to the seat in the same way. It should be fixed a bit lower than the calico so that it covers it completely, which also means that the staples will not conflict. If using braid, apply a continuous bead of glue to the back and, working from the center back, place the braid over the line of staples along the edge of the fabric. Pin to hold it in place until the glue has bonded.

Contemporary dining room

Fabulous contemporary restaurants provide terrific inspiration, and what a tasty way to research a look! The look is essentially pared down, clean, and uncluttered. The materials are natural and the line is simple. With this sensual style, any unnecessary decoration has been removed, to be replaced with space, texture, and clarity.

Some style magazines have named this "hotel chic" and there is an element of truth in the tag. But don't be put off: the hotels they refer to are top-of-the-range, contemporary establishments. They are more like lifestyle palaces where those in the know choose to gather and socialize. Luckily for the rest of us, designs filter down faster than ever now, and most top styles can be recreated and accessorized at a fraction of the original cost. Everyone's doing it, and it's a lot more fun than being conventional. The nine key ingredients include…

Glass

A sheet of tempered, tinted glass resting on a pair of saw horses looks cool and makes a practical dining surface. It is easy to clean, won't scratch, and costs less than wood. Suitable toughened glass with rounded corners and smooth edges can be ordered to size from a local glazier, and several contemporary furniture stores sell pairs of suitable saw horses.

Wood

Dark, stained wood has staged a comeback. If you can't afford the real thing, you can buy a sheet of 1-in. MDF and give it a rosewood finish with the help of some deep, red-brown paint and a rubber graining tool. Supported on saw horses, the finish is amazingly realistic, and if you splash out on a sheet of glass to cover the table top, nobody will be able to tell the difference.

Buying secondhand

Look out for secondhand furniture that can be updated with a dark stain. The lines must be squared off and boxy, with straight or tapered legs. If you have a large room, check out secondhand office furniture dealers, who sometimes have boardroom tables and chairs for sale. This is a way to get top quality furniture at a very low price. And if you're not ready for dark wood or simply prefer a lighter look, then go for pale ash or beech with straight legs and squared-off edges.

Stainless steel

Stainless steel in the dining room is fine in small doses, for example, handles on the sideboard, cutlery, lampshades, and the pepper grinder and saltcellar, otherwise it will begin to look industrial. The trick is to get a balance between the hard and soft edges in the room. Keep it cool but comfortable.

Floors

Carpets are something of a liability when food and wine are being consumed. The best flooring in the contemporary dining room is a floating wooden floor. The least expensive laminated types are fine for a dining room, and are guaranteed to be stain-resistant. If you can't decide between dark and light wood, then why not alternate them? Floor strips laid in stripes of different shades make a really bold, contemporary statement.

The best flooring in a contemporary dining room is a floating wooden floor. The cheapest laminated types are good enough for the dining room; alternated dark and light strips of wood give an effective look.

Chairs

There are many superb modern chairs to choose from, and the key questions to ask are how often you will be using them, and for how many hours at a time. If there are just two of you most of the time, it makes sense to buy two really good chairs and a set of four others that will look good, but which won't break the bank. If you entertain a lot, then bite the bullet and buy a matching set of modern, upholstered chairs because they are definitely the most comfortable.

Children

If children are going to use the dining room every day, the chairs need to be resilient and easy to clean. Shiny wooden floors can be dangerous for children who rock back on their chairs, so fit rubber tips on wooden chair legs or, better still, buy moulded polypropylene or plywood chairs with tubular steel legs, which are always rubber tipped. And, because sitting at the table should never seem like hard work for kids, buy a generous-size, brightly colored PVC cloth to protect the table top so that everyone can relax.

Lighting

The table is the only area that needs to be fully lit. The lighting should be good enough for everyone to see what they're eating without shining in anyone's eyes and blinding them, or being too ambient and not casting enough light. Consider frosted glass wall lights, which can be used to provide an ambient glow, table lamps to add diffused light, and halogen spotlights directed onto the serving area or sideboard. And the table? You can't go wrong with candles. Look for the most contemporary styles, such as long rectangular blocks with six or more wicks, tall tapers, or clear glass tubes. There are so many to choose from.

Color

Choose a harmonious color scheme, avoiding strong contrasts, but this doesn't mean it has to be safe or dull. Textured paint could be applied to one or two walls to give a linen, suede, rustic, or metallic effect. If you are searching for color inspiration, have a look in a contemporary cookbook. A café au lait with a slice of chocolate cake would give you cream, tan, or dark brown, and tandoori chicken with lime pickle and poppadums would give you deep red, burnt orange, and pale yellow. It's not a bad way to plan the dining room color scheme!

A sheet of toughened glass on a saw horse makes a stunning contemporary dining table. The glass can be ordered to size from a glazier, with the corners rounded and the edges smoothed.

THE PROJECTS
The two projects on the following pages show how to make a concealed wall uplighter for subtle, ambient lighting, plus a rosewood-effect dining table out of MDF.

YOU WILL NEED:
- 2 x 1 IN. DAR LUMBER BATTEN FOR WALL FIXING; 24 IN. LONG
- 4 x 1 IN. DAR LUMBER FOR SHELF; 24 IN. LONG
- 6 x ½-IN. MDF FOR FRONT PLATE; 25 IN. LONG
- 4 x ½-IN. MDF, PLUS 2 END PLATES 8 x 4 IN. CUT TO SLOPE BETWEEN THE WALL BATTEN AND THE FRONT PLATE
- 20 ³/₈-IN. SLIM FLUORESCENT LIGHT FITTING AND TUBE
- STRAIGHT EDGE WITH A SPIRIT LEVEL
- PENCIL
- ¹/₈-IN. AND ¹/₄-IN. DRILL BITS
- No. 6 WALL ANCHORS
- No. 6 SCREWS; 1 ⁵/₈ IN. AND 2 IN.

PROJECT ONE
Mood lighting using a concealed uplighter

Instead of buying several feature wall lights, this project shows how to make an uplighter that is fixed on the wall and painted to blend into it. It is in effect an upside-down valance that conceals one or more slimline fluorescent striplights as a low-voltage wall light. Make the box unit to fit the length of wall, or just long enough for a single light fitting (like the fittings usually used below kitchen cupboards). Get a qualified electrician to insert the wiring into the wall; any additional fittings can use the box so that only one wall access point is needed.

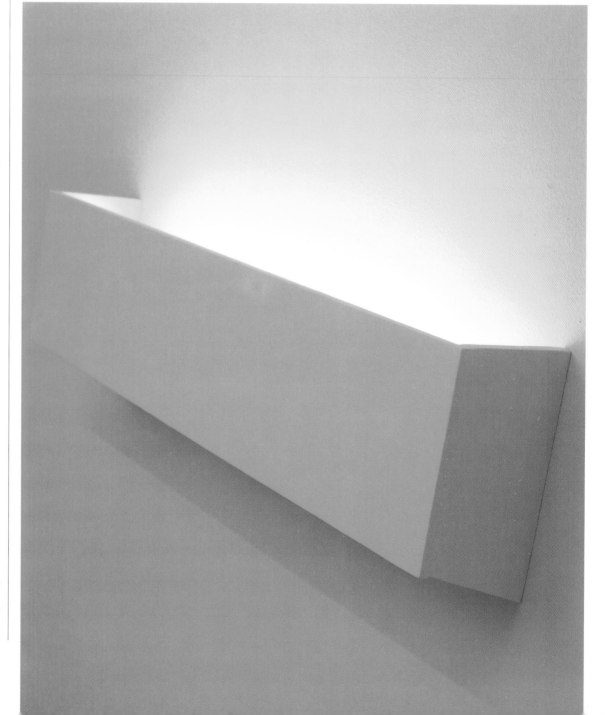

This subtle uplighter is made out of MDF and painted the same color as the wall behind. Behind it is a slimline fluorescent striplight. The uplighter can be made to fit a single light fitting, like this one, or made to fit the length of a whole wall.

HOW TO DO IT

STEP 1 Mark the position for the 2 x 1-in. batten on the wall. Ideally this should be at eye level so that the tubes are completely concealed by the front plate.

STEP 2 Locate the studs in the wall and fix the batten into them using the 2-in. screws.

STEP 3 Fix the shelf to the batten, at a right angle to the wall, using 1 5/8-in. screws.

STEP 4 Place the end plates in position, and mark the angle to be cut away between the front and the batten. Use a saw to cut the angle, then fix the end plates in position.

STEP 5 Fix the MDF front plate to the shelf front using a 1 5/8-in. screw every 4 in.

STEP 6 Prime the unit, then paint it using the same color as the wall behind. Place the light fitting inside the unit and connect the wiring as necessary. There is no need to fix the light fitting inside the unit.

PROJECT TWO

Rosewood-graining an MDF table top

Rosewood has a deep red base with a dramatic near-black grain. The real thing is very expensive, but it is actually quite easy to fake with the aid of a rubber graining roller. This can be bought in specialized paint stores and even some hardware chainstores. MDF is an ideal material for this treatment because it has a perfectly smooth surface with no grain of its own. Buy a sheet of 1-in. MDF cut to a size that will suit your room and the number of people you need to seat, and support it on saw horses. If you have never tried woodgraining before, don't be put off, it is not as technical as it appears. You will need to practice with the graining tool and glaze, however, before you paint the table. You will soon discover the right amount of glaze needed and the technique for rocking the roller as you go.

This rosewood-effect dining table has been made using MDF, a rubber graining roller, and a deep-red vinyl silk paint.

HOW TO DO IT

STEP 1 Paint the table top and edges with a coat of diluted PVA, 3 parts glue to 1 part water, to seal the surface.

STEP 2 Apply a coat of the red base color and leave it to dry. Check for coverage and, if it needs one, apply a second base coat.

STEP 3 Mix up the glaze using 4 parts glaze to 1 part black paint.

STEP 4 Paint the glaze over the red base coat using a flat-ended paint brush. Gently wipe the cotton cloth over the wet surface so that only the thinnest layer of glaze remains. Don't scrub it all off, and leave a fine film of glaze for the graining.

STEP 6 Do the edges of the table top in exactly the same way. Leave the graining to dry, and then apply two coats of clear matte varnish.

STEP 5 Hold the graining roller with both hands, with the ridges curving down. Beginning at one end, hold the roller on the glazed surface and gently pull it toward you, rolling it over as you go. Having reached the extremity, begin rocking it back the other way, still pulling it toward you. Continue to the end, and begin again alongside the first strip.

Sitting-dining room

The large room with a dining area at one end and the sitting area at the other has been around for a very long time. Large Victorian and 1900s houses often featured tall folding doors between the reception rooms, to be opened up for large social gatherings. The open-plan lifestyle came in with the 1960s and, by the end of the 1970s, there were not many downstairs dividing walls left standing. For many years now new houses have been built to an open-plan design downstairs, to make them feel as spacious as possible. Recent trends have seen the dining area become more defined, with low walls, glass bricks, and screens being used to reinforce the fact that the room serves two different purposes.

Lighting is one way of subtly separating the eating from the seating areas. The sitting area needs relaxed lighting with table lamps or wall lights, while the dining table can be lit from above.

The seating and eating areas should ideally complement each other while being divided into separate areas. There are a number of ways to achieve this effect. Five areas you need to look at include:

Color

When choosing the color for the dining end of your room, you must look at the room as a whole, which means taking all the existing colors into account. The furniture, curtains, carpets, and paintings at one end must not look out of place with what you choose for the other. One of the projects in the following section shows how to use the same background color throughout, and then mask off sections of wall and paint blocks of a deeper, more intense version of the same color. This gives the dining area a different character while retaining a harmonious color scheme. For a more dramatic effect, use the same technique but with blocks of contrasting color.

Lighting

Clever lighting alone can define the different areas and make the same color look warmer, cooler, brighter, or more faded. The sitting area needs to have a relaxing atmosphere, which can be achieved with table lamps, wall lights, and accent lights directed onto your favorite things. The dining table can be lit from above with a track of halogen spotlights, a chandelier, or candelabra, depending upon the furniture style.

Flooring

One of the clearest ways of saying this end is for comfort and the other is for eating, is to have different types of flooring. This could be linoleum or a floating wooden floor at one end, and a fitted carpet at the other. If this idea sounds too fixed, then consider fitting one type of flooring throughout, and using a large round rug as the focus point in the sitting room.

Screening

A screen describes a barrier other than a wall—it could be solid and transparent, such as a glass brick wall, or something that you can see through, like cube shelving or a line of wooden rods. A semi-sheer curtain on a decorative rail (as shown in one of the following projects) is a good compromise because it can be drawn to section off the dining area for special occasions, and when drawn back softly frames both sides.

Furniture and accessories

Dining furniture for a dual-purpose room should be lighter and more compact than something for a dining room. Choose a square or circular table with extra flaps or panels so that it can expand when necessary and not be too obtrusive at other times. A sideboard is ideal in a room like this, because the plates, glasses, and cutlery can be hidden away conveniently close to the table. After years in the furniture wilderness, the sideboard is now an absolute "must-have" in contemporary homes.

THE PROJECTS

The two projects on the following pages show subtle yet effective ways of separating the eating from the seating areas of a sitting-dining room. The first, a semi-sheer curtain divider, is the modern equivalent of 1900s or Victorian folding doors between reception rooms. The second project shows how to use color-blocking to separate the two areas while keeping the same color scheme throughout the room. Incorporate your personal style in the colors you choose.

Tables in sitting-dining rooms need to be lighter and more compact than those in separate dining rooms, so they are not too obtrusive over the whole area.

YOU WILL NEED:

- STEEL CURTAIN RAIL
  (SUITABLE FOR
  CEILING MOUNTING)
- DRILL
- STRING AND
  PAINTER'S TAPE
- CAVITY WALL
  ANCHORS
- FABRIC

PROJECT ONE
Curtain divider

The treatment you choose for your sitting or dining room must reflect your own lifestyle. There is little point in having a semi-sheer curtain divider if you also own a large, boisterous dog, no matter how much you like the idea! And avoid any fabric with too much bulk, because the best curtains should hang as flat panels without any gathering. Embroidered sari fabric will give an exotic look, while muslin is modern and minimalist, but you could also use a light cotton canvas as a flat "wall" of color.

This curtain divider will subtly divide the seating and eating areas in a sitting-dining room. The best materials to use are light, so they hang as flat panels without any gathering. Semi-sheer fabric, muslin, embroidered sari fabric, or light, cotton canvas are all ideal.

HOW TO DO IT

STEP 1 Measure an equal distance from the dining end to the center of the room on opposite walls, and mark these points on the baseboard in pencil.

STEP 2 Use a line plumbed to the baseboard. Take a vertical measurement up to the ceiling height (using a straight edge with a spirit level) and make a pencil mark. Run a length of string across the ceiling between the two marks to be a guideline for the rail fitting.

STEP 4 Drill out all the holes for the screws and slide the center fixing onto the rail and screw in position.

STEP 5 Insert the cavity wall anchors. These are specially designed with claws to grip wallboard from the back as the screws go in.

STEP 6 Clip the curtain rings onto the fabric, or slip the curtain header tabs onto the rail.

STEP 3 Mark the positions for the screws to hold the rail fittings. The rails are supplied with fittings, usually one at each end with one in the middle.

YOU WILL NEED:
- PAINTER'S TAPE
- PLUMB LINE
- STRAIGHT EDGE
- SET SQUARE
- PENCIL
- TEST POTS (LATEX, METALLICS, OR TEXTURED PAINTS)
- PAINT BRUSH
- WALLPAPER PASTE IF COLOR-WASHING

PROJECT TWO

Color-blocking

The wonderful thing about this decorating idea is that you can use test pots for all the feature colors. The base color is applied throughout the whole room, then the dining area is enlivened with blocks of color. This can be done in all sorts of ways, using different colors and textures. A multicolored wall of squares, a graduated color change from left to right, or deeper, more saturated shades of the background color are some different types of ideas to try. Contrasts in texture are important too, and can be introduced with metallic paints, chalky distempers, or by thinning the latex paint with wallpaper paste to make a transparent glaze.

The wall of this dining area is decorated in multicolored squares, but the color scheme of the whole room is the same. You can introduce contrasts in texture by using metallic, chalky, or glazed paint.

HOW TO DO IT

STEP 1 Having decided upon the shape, size, and position of the squares on the wall, mark the verticals along the baseboard in pencil (for instance, 12 in. – 6 in. – 12 in. – 6 in.).

STEP 2 Hang the plumb line down the wall as a vertical guide, then use the straight edge and a pencil to make guide marks for the same grid going up the wall (12 in. – 6 in. – 12 in. – 6 in.).

STEP 3 Run tape up from the baseboard in straight lines. Then, using the level to check that the corners are square, run tape horizontally across the wall, intersecting the verticals and completing the grid of squares.

STEP 4 For a color-wash effect, mix wallpaper paste into latex (half and half) and spread the glaze with random brush strokes.

STEP 5 Apply the color of your choice in all the large squares.

STEP 6 Once the paint has dried, carefully peel off all the painter's tape.

TIP
• You can use metallic paints as well, to catch the light and make the room appear larger. These are now generally available from hardware stores everywhere.

Bedrooms

The bedroom should be a sanctuary, a place of rest, a temple of calm. But since it is also the room least on display to friends, it is easy to pay less attention to bedrooms than to other rooms. The bedroom has a range of practical functions that need to be taken into account in any redesign. Apart from sleeping, it is a place for storing clothes, getting dressed, styling hair, reading, and perhaps watching television. Children's rooms have another set of functions that need to be taken into account, not least their own preferences. Above all, the fact that bedrooms are the most private rooms in the house means they are the perfect place to express yourself.

Traditional bedroom

Traditional style in the bedroom means grand, comfortable, and irresistible, but certainly not old-fashioned in any way. This is the sort of room where you should feel very grown-up, and since it is also where you do most of your dreaming, it should be the room of your dreams. The star of the show is the bed, which should be as comfortable as your budget allows, with a good bed head, a bedside table for your champagne or morning cup of tea, soft but effective lighting, and twice as many pillows as you really need.

Alcoves are ideal places for shelving, and to position dressing tables and mirrors. Look out for traditional furniture in local auctions.

This style uses lots of traditional ideas—it could be very feminine, with lace, frills, and satin, or have the understated elegance of dark wooden furniture, monogrammed cotton pillowcases, satin-edge blankets, and a cream woven coverlet. And how about a four-poster bed with a plump eiderdown, or a shiny brass bed with a patchwork quilt? Because this is the one room in your house that people visit by invitation only, you can truly please yourself.

A low-ceilinged room would look smaller with a four-poster, but a similar lighter effect can be achieved by fixing curtain rails above the bed hung with muslin or voile drapes. If the idea of being curtained in sounds too claustrophobic, then a canopy on the wall behind the bed head with fabric drapes falling to the floor will frame the bed, giving a romantic but less enclosed look. The canopy can be fixed to something as simple as a wooden shelf fitted with a decorative molding.

You can really work wonders with fabric and a staple gun. Any existing headboard can be revamped with a new fabric cover, and a plain bed can be dressed up with a headboard of MDF covered with upholstery foam and fabric, which is then screwed onto the wall or hung from a curtain pole. Trimmings of fringe, tassels, buttons, ribbons, lace, or fancy braids can be stitched on or attached with a glue gun.

Storage

Unless there is space for a separate dressing room, you will need a wardrobe and drawers for clothes, somewhere for shoes, and perhaps a dressing table. Make use of any alcoves for shelving or hanging space and, if you have a bay window, fit a built-in window seat with lift-off lids covered with cushions to match the bedcover or curtain fabric, and storage space below. If wardrobes are fitted, make sure that they suit the look of the bedroom. Wooden door panels can be removed and replaced with soft panels of gathered fabric on net curtain wires. Visit local furniture auctions, where you can often find traditional bedroom suites. They really don't make furniture the way they used to, except at the top end of the market, but old wooden furniture given a new paint finish and upholstery can look fantastic, and will cost much less than similar new furniture in traditional styles.

Try a stripped pine blanket chest to store out-of-season clothes or, if you've had enough of pine, give it a dark stain or try something like découpage or a crackle-glaze effect. Boxes on casters under the bed are a good place to keep your shoes. But remember that all storage for items currently in use should be easily accessible, otherwise it just doesn't work. If there isn't enough floor space to pull out an underbed drawer, then keep the drawer for things that you won't need for a while.

Walls and floors

Choose colors that are easy on the eye and patterns that won't keep you awake at night. Don't try to match everything, or the result could be a bedroom with no personality. Stripes, checks, and floral patterns can all be combined if the colors are similar, as can different textures like tweed, cotton, velvet, and linen. Don't use too many different colors though; two or three main ones are enough, with accents of contrasting colors in small amounts. Fabric trimmed with a ribbon border can be used on the walls in place of wallpaper, or hung from a picture rail around the bed. Pattern motifs can also be copied from textiles and made into stencils to decorate the walls or furniture. Floors should ideally be soft carpets, but if you prefer wooden floorboards, make sure you have "islands" of soft bedside rugs.

Windows

A traditional bedroom has curtains. Indulge in generous drapes, deep valances, and black-out linings. Generosity is the key, and it is better to use lots of cheap fabric like unbleached calico or suit lining, and dress it up with a boldly contrasting ribbon, or deep fringe border than to use small amounts of an expensive fabric.

Accessories and lighting

Have at least one good mirror on the wall, and for a real touch of luxury, nothing beats a vase of fresh flowers. Think about the practical lighting you need for wardrobes and drawers as well as pretty bedside lighting—if you have an overhead light, use a dimmer switch for a shadowy, sensual atmosphere.

Decluttering

Most of the clutter in the bedroom comes from newspapers, books, shoes, laundry (clean and dirty), make-up, accessories, and jewelry. It helps if

you begin by having a place for everything, then all you have to do is keep up the good work. New stuff arrives all the time, so unless you constantly clear out the unwanted, things will begin to pile up.

Small cupboards

Give a small cupboard a traditional French country look by painting it green, blue, or deep pink, and replace its door panels with chicken wire sprayed to match. Stretch net curtain wires above and below the panels on the back of the doors with screw-in eyelets, and gather fabric panels on to them. Choose a fabric that you already have in the room.

A canopy fixed to the wall behind the bed head with drapes falling either side frames the bed in a romantic look that is less enclosed than the four-poster.

THE PROJECTS
The following projects show how to transform your bedroom into the traditional style using both decorative and functional ways. Some accessories and trimmings should do the rest.

YOU WILL NEED:
- STENCIL CARD
- TRACING PAPER
- SNAP-BLADE KNIFE
- CUTTING MAT OR PIECE OF THICK CARD
- SPRAYMOUNT
- STENCIL BRUSH
- RULE
- PLUMB LINE AND BLUETACK
- TEST POTS OR STENCIL PAINT
- PLATE

PROJECT ONE
Stenciling a wall

Stenciling has been around for a very long time, but not everyone has the confidence to cut out a stencil and paint their bedroom wall. This little stencil motif will get you started, but be warned, once you realize how easy and effective stenciling can be, you won't want to stop! Stencils can be cut from any waxed cardboard or plastic specially formulated for this purpose. The advantage of plastic is that it is transparent and easier to align, but with a simple pattern like this one you can draw a vertical line through it, and visually line it up with a plumb line each time you move it. The pattern is stenciled with a half-drop on each second row.

This simple stencil motif is easy to paint and very effective on a traditional bedroom wall. Choose the stencil paint in your favorite calm color.

HOW TO DO IT

STEP 1 Photocopy or trace the pattern and spray the back of it with Spraymount. Stick it onto the stencil material. Place the stencil material on the cutting mat, and cut out the shape using a snap-blade knife. Peel off the paper and draw a line through the middle as a guide.

STEP 2 Spray the back of the stencil with Spraymount. This will make the stencil sticky enough to stay flat against the wall, and stop the paint from bleeding under the stencil. It will also peel off the wall leaving no residue.

STEP 3 Put some paint onto the plate and load up the stencil brush with paint. Now wipe most of the paint off on a sheet of paper towel (you only need a tiny bit of paint for stenciling).

STEP 4 The first line of stencil pattern is applied in a straight line 12 in. apart. Starting in one corner, fix the plumb line to the top of the wall, measure 12 in. across and down, and line up the top of the stencil. Check the center line with the plumb line, then apply the paint in a light swirling stroke. Begin at the edges and work inward. Don't overdo it, because you can always return to add more paint once it is dry. Complete the first row.

STEP 5 Move the plumb line across and begin the second row 12 in. across from the first, but start this one 6 in. from the top of the wall. Stencil the next motif 12 in. below, and continue in the same way as before. The third row is started 12 in. from the top, and the following one 6 in., and so on.

Enlarge the stencil below and transfer onto plastic or stencil paper. Line up the stencils on the wall, as shown in the second sketch below.

YOU WILL NEED:

- 4 UPRIGHTS; 2 X 2 IN.
- 2 TOP SIDE LENGTHS (MITERED); 2 X 1 IN.
- 2 TOP END LENGTHS (MITERED); 2 X 1 IN.
- 2 LOWER SIDE LENGTHS (MITERED); 1 X ⁵/₈ IN.
- 2 LOWER END LENGTHS (MITERED); 1 X ⁵/₈ IN.
- SAW
- SANDPAPER
- MITER SAW OR BLOCK
- ¹/₈-IN. DRILL BIT
- WOOD GLUE
- 2-IN. NO. 6 SCREWS
- COMBINATION SQUARE
- PENCIL
- SCREWDRIVER
- COUNTERSUNK BIT

PROJECT TWO

The four-poster

This project shows you how to build a four-poster frame around a plain bed, and once the frame is in place you can choose a fabric to give the bed the look of your choice—floral chintz for an English country house style, or calico and gingham for an American folk look.

The first key step is to decide the height of your bed, which should relate to the ceiling height in your bedroom, and then follow the simple construction steps. The frame can be painted or varnished, depending upon the style of your room.

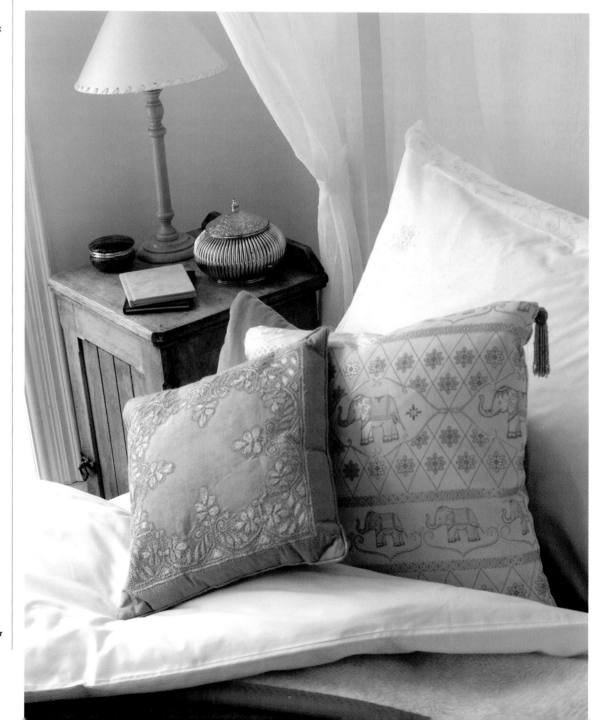

A four-poster frame transforms a bed into the ultimate in romantic decadence. The choice of fabric will give the bed its look—whether it's floral chintz, calico and gingham, or sheer white muslin.

HOW TO DO IT

STEP 1 Measure the length of the bed base and add 4 in. to allow for the width of the uprights. Miter the top and lower side lengths to this measurement. Measure the width of the bed base, and miter the top and lower end pieces to this measurement. Sandpaper all the cut edges.

STEP 2 The top ends and sides are fitted flush with the top of the uprights. To find the height for the broad lower planks surrounding the bed, measure the distance from the floor to halfway up the mattress. This is where the top of the lower planks are fixed to the uprights.

STEP 3 Make up the bed ends first. Lay down parallel one set of uprights, with the top and lower end lengths between them. Drill holes for two screws at each joint. Apply wood glue and screw the pieces together. Repeat to make up the other bed end.

STEP 4 Drill and countersink screw holes in all the top and lower side pieces, and pilot holes in the uprights, making sure that these screws will miss the ones already located there.

STEP 5 The top sides can now be screwed in place, with your assistant supporting one end while you stand on a stepladder and secure the other. The completed bed frame can be painted, stained, or varnished, and hung with tab-top curtains.

STEP 6 This is where you need an assistant—ask a friend for help, or prop one frame end against the wall with the bed pushed against it. Support the lower sides at the foot end while screwing them to the uprights at the head end. Have your assistant hold the foot end upright while you screw the lower sides to it.

TIP
• If you prefer a more gathered curtain effect, fit a standard curtain rail to the inside edge of the top frame and hang the curtains from it in the usual way.

PROJECT THREE
Dressing table with storage space below

A plain table with a shelf below can be easily converted into a dressing table and storage area with the help of fabric, Velcro, a sheet of glass, and a free-standing mirror. Once you've made the floor-length fabric skirt for the table, add lace, ribbon, or braid edging, and top it with a sheet of toughened, smooth-edged glass ordered to size from your local glazier.

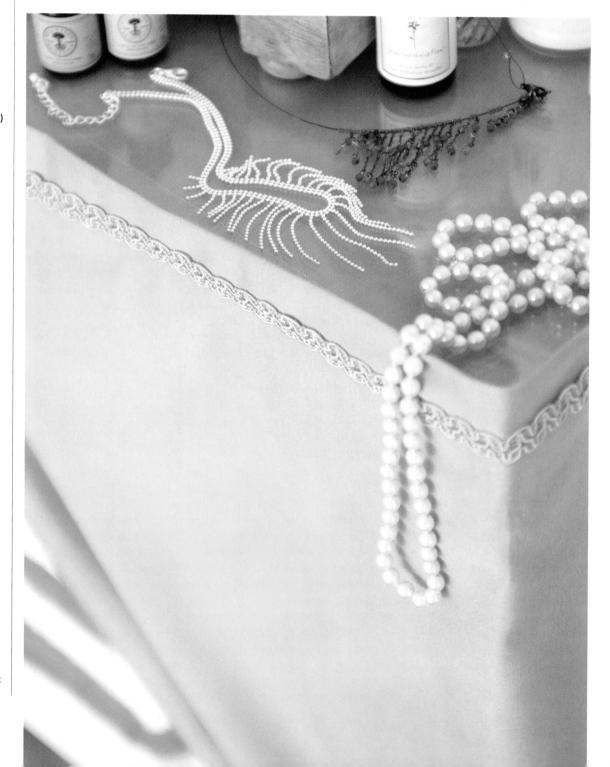

A plain table with a shelf beneath can be easily transformed into a traditional dressing table, with useful storage for the less attractive cosmetic bottles and tubes you'd rather not have on display.

HOW TO DO IT

STEP 1 Measure the height from the table top to the floor, and then measure around the sides and the front, adding a bit extra for an overlap. If you want to pleat the "skirt", then allow more fabric. Divide the length into two.

STEP 2 Depending upon the condition of the table top, either cover it with fabric or a lace cloth, or paint or stain it with the color of your choice.

STEP 3 Stick the looped side of the Velcro around the table edge.

STEP 4 Turn back a hem on the top and bottom of the skirt, and sew or bond with iron-on tape.

STEP 5 Sew or stick the other side of the Velcro tape to the top hem of the fabric. Press the skirt onto the table edge. Have one piece overlap the other by about 3/4 in. where they meet in the middle. Fix a small square of looped Velcro to fasten the overlap. And finally, place the glass on the table top. Add a vase of flowers and a mirror, and hide all your undesirables behind the curtain!

Contemporary bedroom

There are many different ways to create a contemporary look, but the style is predominantly about clean lines, clear space, and creating an atmosphere. This is the age of the senses, where aromatherapy and Feng Shui are considered mainstream, and natural colors, fabrics, and decorating materials are understood to bring a feeling of well-being. Minimalism has been the biggest recent influence on home decorating, and the quickest way to get the contemporary look is to clear the surfaces, put away all your clutter, lay a wooden floor, and light some candles.

Efficient storage is a must in the contemporary bedroom. It is the only way to keep clothes, shoes, cosmetics, and jewelry out of sight and maintain the minimalist style. Ideally, clothes would be stored in a separate dressing room, freeing up the bedroom space of functional furniture, but in reality few of us have this choice, so we have to be creative with our storage options. Five key things to consider when creating a contemporary bedroom include...

Ideally, the only furniture in a contemporary bedroom is the bed. Walk-in wardrobes or separate dressing rooms are an effective luxury that keep the bedroom clutter-free.

Furniture

The double bed is a very big piece of furniture that will immediately dominate the room. If you give the bed a contemporary makeover, then the rest of the room can follow. If you already have a good bed, then it is worth keeping because beds are very expensive. Give it a change of style by adding a drop-in headboard, one of the projects in this section.

Pine bed heads with turned spindles were very popular, but now look very dated. They can be boxed in with sheets of MDF or plywood, and painted or covered with foam and fabric to make a really comfortable back rest. Basic upholstery like this can be tackled with a staple gun, double-sided tape, and a glue gun. Stick the foam to the MDF, staple the fabric over the top of it, and neaten the edges with a plain ribbon trimming stuck on with the hot glue gun. You can do it!

An alternative plain and minimal style is the Japanese look. If your budget is tight, and you don't mind sleeping on a futon, then you can make a really cheap and stylish bed base out of a pair of wooden pallets. The wood will need sanding to get rid of potential splinters, and then you just put the futon on top. Keep bedside tables low, place woven grass mats on each side of the bed, fit paper shades and blinds, and hang framed Japanese prints on the walls.

If you are starting from scratch, then go for a low-level platform bed with built-in storage below and reading lights in the headboard. There are some amazing new wooden beds around that have a wardrobe's worth of drawers built in, but be warned, because they are very expensive. Iron bed frames are cool and popular, and there are loads of original designs made by small companies. Look for individual makers in magazine small ads if you are looking for something unique. They are also made in different finishes, aluminum being one of the latest styles, and all the big furniture stores have their own ranges of metal beds. If you choose one, be sure to have plenty of pillows because they are cold and hard to lean against.

The Shaker style is now making a comeback, even though it's over 250 years since it first appeared in America (the Shakers were an offshoot of the Quakers). The Shakers lived in community houses without any unnecessary decoration or personal possessions, keeping the floor space clear and putting everything away in built-in cupboards. All of these ideas strike a minimalist chord, and the furniture is so beautiful that the reproduction Shaker style is now one of the most popular styles around.

Wardrobes and chests of drawers are large enough to ruin any sense of space you create with careful use of lighting and color, so think carefully whether you really need them. If you only have skirts, shirts, and pants to hang up, then fit double rods in a small wardrobe and use the full height of it. Space below hanging clothes can so easily become untidy, so put in a shoe rack or storage boxes. Also check out new wardrobes with frosted glass doors, but be aware that they will only look good if everything inside is tidy.

If you are lucky enough to have a big room, think about having a false wall built to make a

You can't go wrong with white as a color scheme—it reflects the light, is flattering to the complexion, and goes with everything. Off-whites look particularly good with wood.

If you've got windows to flaunt, make the most of them by fitting blinds into the window recesses, or make them more dramatic with floor-to-ceiling billowing muslin drops.

walk-in wardrobe. This need not use up more than 3 ft. of room space (including the partition wall). This storage space is just right for all your clothes and shoes, suitcases, and spare bedding. The only furniture needed in the bedroom would be the bed. Now that is luxury!

The way you decorate the bedroom windows depends on several things. Do you need to keep out drafts or traffic noise? Does the sun shine too brightly in the morning? Are the window frames attractive, and do you have a nice view? Try thick curtains for absorbing noise and blocking drafts, making the room a lot more cosy. For a warm, contemporary style, use blankets, felt, or lined fleece to make curtains. Block out the sun with black-out lining material, which costs a bit more than ordinary lining, but really is effective. If the window frames are a good feature, like the old wooden double-hung kind, they shouldn't be hidden away, and you can fit blinds into the window recess. There are some fabulous new materials and designs, including felt and denim for warmth, voile to allow the light in, pierced patterns, and lots of variations on the classic Venetian blind.

Color schemes

Bedroom color schemes need to create a mood. A natural palette of greens, browns, and off-whites looks fabulous with wood. It is a sophisticated choice and these colors are also harmonious and relaxing. If you feel a bit wilder, there are some wonderful, rich colors to choose from. Bedroom colors can also be toned down or livened up for a change of mood by using the right lighting. Lilac, turquoise, and pink are a wonderfully feminine combination with a contemporary edge, while cinnamon, oatmeal, mushroom, and chocolate brown are warm, rich, masculine colors. Blue is spacious and dreamy, and white reflects the light, flatters the complexion, and goes with virtually everything.

Lighting

Bedroom lighting can be divided into three definite areas. The room as a whole might need a large, central chandelier-type light fitted with a dimmer switch. The bedside area needs reading lights, while task lighting will help you find things in the wardrobe after dark. Choose lights that switch on when you open the door, or simple, battery-powered lights for occasional use.

Flooring

The flooring for the contemporary bedroom is best kept plain. If you have wooden floorboards, paint them with wood wash that is a lighter version of one of the colors used in the room. Pale wooden floors look good, and soft rugs can be used by the bedside to warm your toes in the morning.

Decorating this room is really very personal. It's a place to enjoy being wrapped in those colors, textures, and patterns that please you. And whatever you do, never sacrifice comfort for style in the bedroom.

Decluttering

Clutter can be everything. It's the mail that arrives in the morning that sits next to the tea things by the nail varnish and the hair slides, with the case for your eyeglasses and the pen by the notepad right next to the phone. And sometimes it threatens to engulf us. When this point is reached, it is time for some serious decluttering.

Try to clear the morning clutter when you leave the bedroom. Have a deep-sided tray for the morning tea or coffee, and make sure that the mail, newspapers, and glasses from the night before are taken out there and then. Look out for a stylish bed tray or breakfast tray—they have two side compartments that act as legs with a sturdy section across the middle. A bedside magazine rack is a necessity, and once you have one you may wonder why they are not considered standard bedroom accessories. Also buy matching boxes in a range

of sizes—choose leather, wicker, clear acrylic, or canvas. Mount bookshelves on the wall in an alcove, or as a series of modular cube shelving units. Keep videos in a box with a lid, because even if they are neatly stacked, their packaging still looks like clutter. Buy a wooden ladder to lean up against the wall—use a dark wood stain to smarten it up, and use it as a temporary resting place for discarded clothes and towels. Buy a laundry basket and waste paper basket to match the room style, and finally an open shoe rack big enough for the shoes you wear all the time, keeping out-of-season and special occasion pairs stacked in matching shoe boxes. Decluttering is all about learning to be organized and stylish at the same time.

The natural colors of wood and the stone flooring, with the clean, clutter-free lines of built-in wardrobes, give this bedroom a contemporary look.

THE PROJECTS
The two projects on the following pages suggest how to start achieving a contemporary look in your own bedroom. A fresh coat of paint, some flexible lighting, and some disciplined decluttering should do the rest.

YOU WILL NEED

- WOOD AS FOLLOWS:
  1 BACK ³/₄-IN. MDF,
  1 SHEET OF 8 x 4 FT.;
  1 TOP SHELF DAR
  SOFT WOOD, 5³/₄ IN.
  x 8 FT.;
  2 SIDES ³/₄-IN. MDF,
  48 x 24 IN. (SEE PLAN
  FOR CUT-OUT);
  2 INNER SIDES ³/₄-IN.
  MDF, 19 x 24 IN.;
  2 SHELVES ³/₄-IN.
  MDF, 19 x 17 IN.;
  2 TOPS ³/₄-IN. MDF,
  19 x 19¹/₂ IN.
- BOX OF TWIN-
  THREAD 2-IN.
  No. 6 SCREWS
- WOOD GLUE
- WOOD FILLER
- SANDPAPER
- PRIMER AND
  SEMIGLOSS PAINT
- DRILL WITH
  COUNTERSINK, ¹/₈-IN.
  PILOT HOLES AND
  SCREWDRIVER BIT
- LONG RULE
- COMBINATION
  SQUARE
- PENCIL
- TAPE MEASURE
- SMALL FOAM ROLLER
  AND TRAY

PROJECT ONE
A drop-in bed surround

Building a box headboard with a shelf and two side tables sounds ambitious, but be assured, it is totally simple, and the construction method is quite straightforward. It can be done with the most basic tool kit and it will make the bedroom look utterly chic.

The list on the left gives the sizes of all the pieces of MDF and softwood needed to make this surround to fit a 60-in.-wide double bed. Most lumber merchants will cut the wood to size for a small fee, which will save time considering the number of different lengths needed.

This stunning bed surround is practical as well as chic. It can be an effective way of boxing in the now-dated pine bed heads, and you can either leave the surrounds painted or attach basic upholstery.

HOW TO DO IT

STEP 1 Cut out the waste from the two ends and sand the edges.

STEP 2 Draw positional guides for the assembly of the sides, back, and inner sides. Mark these very carefully with pencil lines.

STEP 3 Drill pilot holes for the screws and countersink them.

STEP 4 Screw the sides and inner shelves to the back.

STEP 5 Add the shelves and the tops.

STEP 6 Fill and sand the countersink holes. Seal, prime, and paint.

> **TIP**
> • Unpainted MDF looks good varnished. If you don't intend to paint it, then use brass screws with screw-cup washers rather than countersunk screws. They will be a visible feature and look better than patches of wood filler.

Use this sketch to help you position the surround correctly around your bed. You will need an assistant to help you drop it in place against the wall.

PROJECT TWO

Using textures to create a comfort zone

YOU WILL NEED:

- 6 FT. CORDUROY
  FABRIC
- 60 IN. ARTIFICIAL
  FUR FABRIC
- 60 IN. OF 4.5 OZ.
  QUILT WADDING
- PINS
- THREAD
- SEWING MACHINE

Most of the time we spend in the bedroom is in darkness, and this makes it perfect for exploring the use of different textures. These must change with the seasons if they are to be fully appreciated. Imagine stepping out of bed on a hot summer night onto cool, woven grass matting or onto a thin sheepskin fleece in winter. The summer bedroom should be airy, with billowing muslin at the windows and cool cotton sheets on the bed. In winter the bed is more of a cosy nest, with knitted hot-water-bottle covers, soft velvet cushions, thick blankets, and flannel sheets. This bed cover, which is 50 per cent throw and 50 per cent quilt, combines two contrasting textures, corduroy and fake fur, to give 100 per cent comfort! Choose a wonderfully soft and warm fabric such as artificial fur, fleece, or the more hard-wearing corduroy.

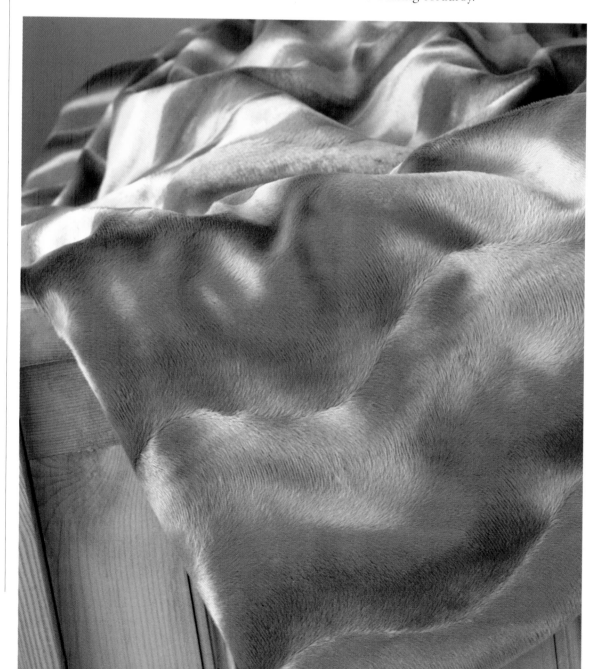

This bed cover combines fake fur on one side with corduroy on the other, each sandwiching quilt wadding, to create the ultimate winter warmer.

HOW TO DO IT

STEP 1 Lay the corduroy on a flat surface with the wadding and fur fabric placed on the top. Place the two top fabrics 2 in. inside the top edge and on one side edge of the cord.

STEP 2 Trim away the fur on the other two sides to make a 2-in. border all round.

STEP 3 Miter the corners. When you fold them over, the two edges meet to make a neat finish.

STEP 4 Fold the fur border over and pin it to the cord. Set the sewing machine to satin stitch, and sew all around the edge and up the middle of the miters so that all the cut edges are sealed and sewn.

TIP
• The choice of feature fabric is up to you, it could be velvet, corduroy, brushed cotton, or even a knitted blanket. Check that the textures will be good companions when you choose them.

Teenage boy's room

Forget about the stereotypical messy teenage boy, he's an urban myth. Boys want to live in nice surroundings just as much as girls do. They have strong ideas about color, fashion, and relaxation, and will not thank you for making these decisions for them. Good TV decorating programs appeal to young people's imaginations, especially with their rule-breaking ideas. It may seem like a contradiction, but being seen as an individual matters just as much to a teenager as being in fashion. And who wants to do things the traditional way when you can get the same effect with panel adhesive in a fraction of the time? Unfortunately what goes up will probably need to come down at some time, and this is where screws have the advantage over glues.

Get teenagers involved in any redecorating from the start. They'll have strong ideas about the colors and style they want, and you might even get them to help...

Start the project with a conference. Decorating influences can come from all over the place—sport, music, fashion, and movies are the four most obvious ones and a good starting point. One way to do something original and fashionable is to mix ideas and decorate using the key features of recognisable brands of clothing. Think trainers, skateboard, surfing, snowboard, and other sports gear with a distinctive style, and you'll be on the right track. If he is into surfing, make a stencil of the logo on his surfboard. It doesn't have to be too literal, just the colors of a brand will be enough to make the statement.

So far it's easy, but the difficulty lies in keeping his enthusiasm alive during the boring preparatory stages. It is hard to be too enthusiastic about primers, undercoats, and filling, so you may have to resort to a good old-fashioned bribe. Try offering a coveted CD to listen to while working, or a new duvet cover, a cool bedside light, or a full-length mirror when the room is finished.

Color can affect moods, so try and talk him out of black walls because they are seriously depressing. And the advantage of another color is that it can always be painted over (unlike black). Just go with the flow! If the room is small, it's a good idea to paint the furniture the same color as the walls, and this is a good way to update wardrobes and chests of drawers that have been around for a while. Whatever the room's dimensions, he will want to have friends stay over. A sofa-bed is ideal, but alternatives include a bed in a bag, a rolled-up camping mat that doubles as a bolster, or a foam cube that unfolds to become a single mattress. A sleeping bag rolled up and tied with a belt makes a pretty good cushion, too.

Homework area

If the room is going to be used for schoolwork, it is important to make it easy for him to study. We all work in different ways, but an organized work area is always helpful. Even if he reads the books sprawled out on the floor, it is better if they are kept on a shelf rather than under the bed. And either buy a desk or build a work table with shelving and a good light source. Make it big enough for a computer, television, and stereo as well, then buy him a swivel chair and he can really get down to business.

There is one more thing that every teenager needs, regardless of his or her interests, and that is a huge noticeboard—kill two birds with one stone by covering a wall or all the walls with softboard. This is the material used to line school corridors so that work can be pinned up. It can be painted to look like any other wall, and used to display anything and everything. It is also great at noise reduction. It should be compulsory!

When it comes to flooring, it is best to choose something that won't stain but will be as soundproof as possible. A good padding will block out most of the beat from his stereo, and carpet tiles are good because they can be lifted and replaced if damage occurs. Hardboard is cheap and under-used as a flooring material. It can be laid in large sheets fixed down with lines of domed upholstery studs, and painted with floor paint to give a hard-edged industrial look. And if the floor is hard, make sure he also has a big soft rug to laze about on—because that's what he'll like best.

THE PROJECTS

The two projects on the following pages give street cred to functional bedroom furniture. The first project shows how to make a bed head out of scaffolding poles, while the second adds a hip-hop stencil to transform a cheap desk.

Traditional American culture is a firm favorite among teenagers, and if you're going to take it on, like this floor-to-ceiling mural, you've got to think big!

PROJECT ONE

The scaffolding pole bed head

This project takes the construction site into the bedroom by using scaffolding poles to make a bed head. You can also make a hanging rail in a similar way. There are companies who specialize in scaffolding beds and platforms, but this project uses galvanized scaffolding materials, bought from a builder's suppliers, to make a serious, industrial-chic statement. A piece of coarse cotton or linen make a comfortable back rest. The items in the list on the left are for a single bed.

This industrial bed head is made out of scaffolding poles, with a section of denim for a back rest. This heavy bed head will need screwing into the floor due to its weight, so make sure you are able to do this before you start.

HOW TO DO IT

STEP 1 Slot the elbow fittings on to the end of one of the cross-pieces and add two 20-in. uprights. Fit the T fittings on to the other cross-piece and fit it on to the uprights. Don't tighten anything up yet.

STEP 2 Wrap the fabric around the two cross-pieces and mark the position for a joining seam at the back with chalk.

STEP 3 Fold the seam over at the back and sew it flat with a double row of stitching.

STEP 4 Loosen the joints at one side and slip the fabric over the two cross-pieces. Tighten up the fittings with the hex key.

STEP 5 Complete the bed head by adding the two lower poles and the end fittings.

STEP 6 This very heavy bed head has to be well secured. Fit the poles into two end plates and screw them to the floor using large screws. And do check that there no water pipes passing underneath the fixing points!

PROJECT TWO

Customizing a cheap computer desk in the hip-hop style

Everyone needs somewhere to work, but that doesn't mean it has to look boring and worthy. This project takes a really inexpensive, white-laminated, fiberboard desk and gives it street cred. The numerals could be exchanged for letters done in the same shadowed style, and whatever pattern you choose, remember it doesn't matter if it's slightly off-center or if the spray drifts a bit at the edges—it'll still look good.

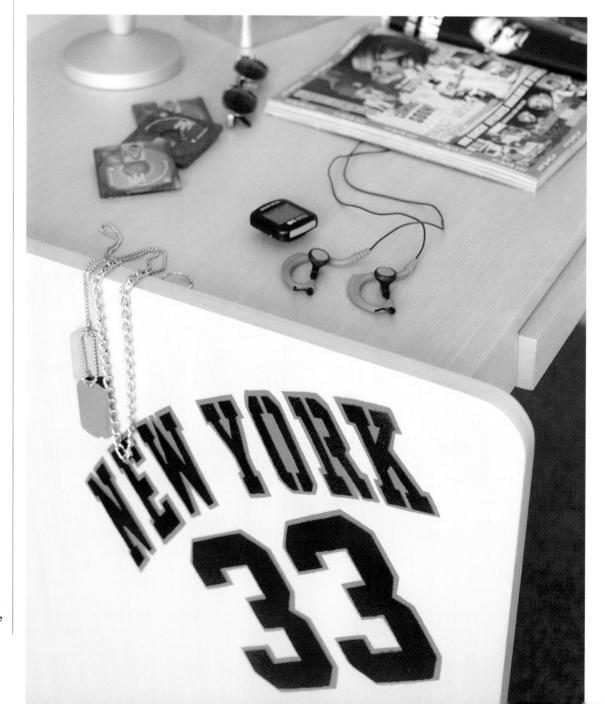

A basketball-style stencil has transformed this inexpensive, white, fibreboard desk. Add stickers, labels, and logos to complete the look.

HOW TO DO IT

STEP 1 Take a photocopy from a favorite sports sweatshirt.

STEP 2 Enlarge the numerals to about 12 in. in length and transfer the patterns onto the stencil card. Cut out two stencils. One should just be the letter outline, the other should have stencil bridges added on letters such as Os and Rs to keep the shape intact.

STEP 3 Use a craft knife to cut out the stencils. Spray the back with Spraymount. One stencil is for the main motif, the other for the border.

STEP 4 Protect a well-ventilated area with lots of newspaper, and then roller or brush the aluminum paint onto the desk.

STEP 5 Attach the first stencil to the desk with painter's tape. Spray this with your first chosen color.

STEP 6 Spray through the second stencil in the second color to create the border. Repeat this as many times as you like on the top, the outsides and insides, and then add as many stickers, logos, and labels as you like.

Teenage girl's room

Decorating is influenced by changes in fashion, and never more so than in a teenage girl's room. The big problem is that fashion is an industry, and in order to keep it ticking over looks have to change with the seasons. What is totally "in" now might be totally "out" in six months' time. Do not despair, though, there are a few hardy perennials that manage to stay cool throughout, and denim tops the chart. The blue denim theme runs through all the projects in this section, but apart from the cushion cover made from old jeans, the same methods could be used to suit different fabrics.

Plan any bedroom makeover together, and make sure she gets to choose the style. If you absolutely hate the combinations she chooses, you could always try reverse psychology and pretend it was exactly what you were thinking for the room too...

If this is the first major makeover since childhood, take time to plan the decorating together. If you're stuck for inspiration, then watch TV decorating programs and look through magazines, color charts, and fabric samples. Leaving the toys and other childhood paraphernalia behind is a big step in a girl's life. It can be a bit much if everything familiar and comforting is suddenly whisked away before you're ready to say goodbye so, whatever you do, don't make big changes when she's not there.

A teenager's bedroom is much more than somewhere to sleep. It is a room to entertain friends, experiment with clothes and make-up, listen to music, and study. Planned well, it can be all these things and more. A good way of planning room space is to cut out paper versions of all the furniture and move it around on a room plan. Do this to scale using squared paper, and draw in all the fixed features, like radiators, windows, doors, chimney breasts, alcoves, and any built-in wardrobes or shelves. If the room is small, a platform bed with a desk underneath may be ideal. These used to be too rickety for older children, but they are now being made in stronger materials. They are a brilliant solution if space is limited, because all the sleep and study space is fitted into a compact area, and the rest of the room can be geared toward leisure.

Dressing table

A dressing table is not strictly necessary, but will be appreciated. There is no point in denying it, most girls need somewhere to keep a lot of nail polish, make-up, and hair-styling equipment. They also need mirrors—a long one to see the whole picture, and a small one for close-ups. She will be the envy of all her friends if you wall-mount a mirror surrounded by light bulbs in the film star's dressing-room style—use low-watt, soft-glow type bulbs.

Clothes will pile up on anything that stands still, and a small clothes rail on casters is a really good idea, even if there is a perfectly good wardrobe in the room. This is more like the rail a model would have backstage, with a selection of outfits for the catwalk. Encourage her to keep her school clothes on the rail at night instead of on the floor, and to keep other clothes on the rail or in the wardrobe the rest of the time.

If, like most teenage girls, she likes to dance, you could divide the floor space in two and have carpet in one half and laminated wooden floorboards in the other. This only works in a medium-to-large room, and a small room would look bigger and better with a laminated floor and rugs. If there is going to be music and dancing, don't scrimp on the padding—whatever flooring you choose, this will act as soundproofing.

Color

Wall colors are a personal choice, and the best thing is to step back and only offer your opinion if you're asked for it. If you absolutely hate the combinations she chooses, then you could try reverse psychology and pretend that it's exactly what you had in mind for the dining room! If that doesn't cause an instant rethink, bear in mind that in the end it's only paint, and mistakes can always be put right with a coat of something less alarming.

The style of window treatment will very much depend on the overall look of the room—if she likes the ethnic look, then something floaty like sari fabric would be lovely. A trip to a market is always fun, and they are often a good place to buy ethnic accessories like lamps, cushions, and throws. If she prefers a more contemporary, cool look, then blinds are the best bet. If you don't live near any trendy furniture stores, blinds can be bought by mail order and come in a wide range of materials, including denim and felt.

A new set of bed linen also works wonders, and she'll be spoilt for choice. There are colors and patterns to suit every style and mood, so be adventurous and investigate all the possibilities before making a decision.

Storage

Storage is far less of a nightmare than it used to be, because there are so many good systems on the market. They range from matching boxes that take everything from CDs to shoes, to modular storage cubes that can be added to if you need more space, to wire basket wardrobe organizers with stacks of drawers on casters. Send for all the catalogs (we have a list at the back of the book), then set yourselves a budget and take your pick. Shelves are always a good idea, and a high shelf on one wall makes a good retirement home for all those cuddly toys from childhood.

Lamps

Lamps are now fashionable accessories, having crossed over from furniture stores to gift stores. They are sold alongside novelty greetings cards, cushions, and candles. Young consumers are well aware of the latest trends, and a wacky bedside lamp is rated as a top birthday or Christmas present. On a more practical level, think about getting an anglepoise lamp for studying, and a wardrobe light. Finally, when all the hard work is done and the room looks out of this world, step back and let her take the credit for everything. It will be worth it!

Alcoves can make interesting spaces for wall-mounted desks and book-shelves, keeping the homework side of the room to a compact corner.

THE PROJECTS
The two projects on the following pages both focus on denim, the fabric that refuses to date, and the ultimate in cool.

PROJECT ONE
Denim tab-top curtains

Tab tops are really easy to make if you have a sewing machine. In fact, sewing is the best way to do it, because denim is a heavyweight fabric, and very difficult to sew by hand. To jazz the denim up, sew a bright button at the bottom of each tab—you could also use metal stars, which are also very "jeans." The curtain rail is a stainless-steel rod, which can be purchased from any hardware store, although you could use copper piping instead. Line the curtains with a lightweight fabric that could be a plain color, gingham, or a floral print.

You can't go wrong with denim tab-top curtains, which are easy to make if you have a sewing machine.

HOW TO DO IT

STEP 1 Cut a 6¼-in.-deep band the width of the fabric for the top of each curtain. Cut two 10 ⅛ x 3 ⅛-in. strips per tab. They are spaced 4 in. apart, so calculate how many you will need for your window. Cut the curtain lengths to the drop, adding ¾ in. for turnover and an 3 ⅛-hem. Pin a ¾-in. seam down the sides.

STEP 2 Stitch the side seams on the sewing machine using the gray thread. Turn over the hem and stitch this in the same way.

STEP 3 Place pairs of tabs together with right sides facing, and stitch a seam on both sides. Turn them inside out and press flat with a hot iron. Fold them in half and press the fold.

STEP 4 Turn the curtains over and lay the tabs on top of the fabric with the raw ends slightly overlapping the top edge. Arrange them so that they are spaced 4 in. apart. Check that the folded ends form a straight line and the tabs are exactly the same length. Make any length adjustments at the other end.

STEP 5 Lay the 6 ¼-in. deep band over the tabs on top of the curtain with the dark side facing upward. Pin it in place, keeping the tabs in their positions sandwiched between the two layers of fabric. Stitch all the way across, ¾ in. inside the top edge. Turn the band over. The tabs are now at the top, fully enclosed in the contrasting band. Turn the edge over and top-stitch the band to the curtain. Sew a bright button on each tab.

YOU WILL NEED:
- 1 PAIR OF OLD JEANS
- BALL-POINT PEN
- RULE
- SCISSORS
- PINS
- SEWING MACHINE WITH NEEDLE FOR DENIM
- STRONG THREAD IN ORANGE OR RED
- POLYESTER STUFFING

PROJECT TWO

Cushion cover from old jeans

This is one way to immortalize your favorite jeans or, if the idea of cutting them up is too painful to contemplate, you could buy a secondhand pair from a thrift shop especially for the job. Extra trimmings can be added to spice the cushion up a bit—try a thick fringe, a broderie anglaise frill, velvet ribbons, or some metal stars.

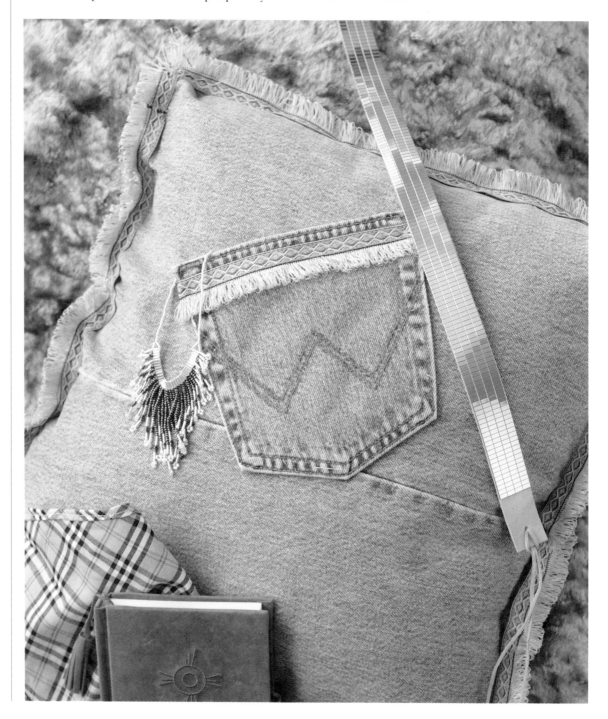

Denim refuses to go away, and fashion designers have given up trying to ignore it, and now bring out new variations, decorations, colors, styles, and hip labels. This cushion cover is made from old jeans.

HOW TO DO IT

STEP 1 Cut the legs of the jeans open along the front. Use a craft knife blade to cut the stitching of the back pockets. Lay the fabric out of a flat surface.

STEP 2 Cut out a square paper pattern and pin this to it. Cut out the two sides of the cushion in this way. Now re-stitch the pockets onto the center of each of the denim squares, using the strong orange or red thread.

STEP 4 Stuff the cushion with the polyester material and slipstitch the seam closed. Sew on any extra trimmings, or pop a remote control into the pocket.

STEP 3 Lay the square down with right sides facing, and pin a seam around the edge. Machine-sew the seam with a double row of stitches, leaving a 4-in. gap open for the stuffing. Snip the corners up to the stitching, and turn the cushion cover the right way out. Press the cushion cover with a hot iron.

YOU WILL NEED:

- ONE VARNISHED WOODEN DINING CHAIR
- PAINT STRIPPER TO REMOVE THE OLD VARNISH
- SCRAPER
- RUBBER GLOVES
- SANDPAPER
- STEEL WOOL
- WHITE WATER-BASE PRIMER
- LIGHT PINK AND DARK PINK LATEX PAINT
- 2-IN. PAINT BRUSH
- 18 IN. FAKE FUR FABRIC
- STAPLE GUN
- FOAM PAD FOR SEAT
- SNAP-BLADE KNIFE
- CARPET-FITTING TAPE
- SPONGE

PROJECT THREE

Pink pony chair

In this project, an old wooden chair is given a funky fur makeover. Old wooden dining room chairs don't cost very much, and you can have a lot of fun searching yard sales for the perfect specimen. Look for a nice-shaped back and a seat that's in good condition.

Give an old dining chair a denim and fake-fur makeover for the ultimate in groovy chic. You could choose denim fabric instead of the fake fur, and paint the chair a denim blue color instead of pink.

HOW TO DO IT

STEP 1 Begin by sanding the chair smooth. Use paint stripper to remove any old paint.

STEP 2 Prime the woodwork of the chair with white water-base primer.

STEP 3 Apply the first coat of the darker pink paint.

STEP 4 Lightly brush the second paler pink color over the top of the first coat.

STEP 5 Gently wipe the paler top coat with a sponge to reveal parts of the dark pink paint.

STEP 6 When the paint is dry, fold brown paper over the seat, creasing at the edges, to make a template.

STEP 7 Cut out the paper template along the creases and place it on the foam pad. Cut round the template with a snap-blade knife.

STEP 8 Lay the paper template on the fur fabric and cut round it, allowing approximately 2 in. for the turnovers.

STEP 9 Cut notches in the fur fabric so that it fits around the curved foam seat pad.

STEP 10 Apply carpet-fitting tape to the foam pad. Peel off the backing.

STEP 11 Press the fur fabric onto the sticky surface, making sure there are no creases.

STEP 12 Stick down alternate notches as you go, easing the fabric around the curved edges.

STEP 13 Apply carpet-fitting tape to the seat of the chair, and stick the covered cushion down.

Children's bedrooms

Decorating a room for a child is brilliant fun. This is where you can experiment with paint effects, use bright colors, and live out all your own childhood fantasies. Whether or not you have a free hand will depend upon the age of your child, but you will know what they like best. All children have strong preferences for particular cartoon characters, animals, activities, and colors from an early age. The best thing is that children love to feel special, and decorating a room especially for them is always a big success.

Children grow out of any cozily decorated nursery quicker than you might expect, but there's more than just redecoration to do to a children's room. Five things to consider when revamping a children's room are...

Decorating

If the room is being re-decorated for the first time since the nursery years, then it is time for a big change. The most obvious, and the cheapest way to change a room is by painting it a fresh, new color. Color is known to affect us psychologically, and this may be worth investigating before you reach for the primary colors. If the room is also going to be a playroom and workroom, then color could be used to separate the areas. Green has calming, reassuring qualities, yellow is sunny, happy, and warm, blue is relaxing and dreamy, and, for obvious reasons, a good ceiling color. Red is far too powerful a wall color for a child's room, but is good for fabrics and features. Boys often like orange, which is said to create a positive atmosphere, and all little girls have a pink phase, which may last for years: in fact some never grow out of it! Also try Roman blinds because they are easy to make, and the design is basic enough to withstand rough treatment. Make them in nice bright fabric backed with black-out lining material so that the room can be darkened for bedtime.

Think about the effect of colors before you choose the wall paint. Yellow is sunny and happy, while blue is relaxing and dreamy. Avoid red walls at all costs!

Play areas

A school-age child will need some sort of work area for model building and painting. Kids need to feel they can relax and make a mess, and that you will not make too much fuss if they spill and scatter things. For this reason it is a good idea to have mess-friendly flooring such as vinyl, linoleum, cork, or laminated floorboards. Two colors of vinyl tiles can be laid as a checkerboard— white with yellow or grey looks good and not too overpowering. This sort of surface is good for all kinds of games as well—wheels speed across it, and handstands can be done without slipping. Mats with a looped pile, more usually seen in the bathroom, are excellent because they come in lovely colors, are non-slip, and can be cleaned in the washing machine. If your child is older and wants a more sophisticated style, then go for cork or laminated floorboards with a soft rug by the bedside, and colorful rugs to laze on.

Lighting

Good lighting is equally important, because children like to see what they are doing clearly. They will also make a lot more mess if they can't find what they're looking for! Lights need to be fixed onto surfaces, otherwise there is the risk that they will be knocked over and cause a fire. Fix anglepoise lights to the worktop or wall above it, simple wardrobe lights that come on when the door is opened, and a wall light above the bed for reading. A central pendant light is a "must" for brightening up the whole room, and small plug-in nightlights can be fitted into the wall sockets to give a soft glow.

Photographs

A frieze of pinboard on one wall will take care of all their favorite cartoon characters, pet pictures, party invitations, paintings, and photographs. A wardrobe door or section of wall could be painted with blackboard paint to make an instant chalkboard. Make it big enough for a few friends to work on at the same time, and supply loads of brightly colored chalks. Also put a nice big mirror on the wall, and buy some easy-access frames so that photographs can be changed from time to time.

Books and toys

Keep bookshelves low down and accessible, but also have high, out-of-reach cupboards for storage. This is especially useful when young children go through the stage of throwing everything out of drawers and cupboards. Buy a set of matching toy boxes on casters, which can be pushed away under the bed or into the bottom of a wardrobe. Also have separate places for paint brushes, construction kits, board games, and dolls with their clothes and accessories. It may sound like hard work, but if everything has a place it is much easier to clear up. You can even try a row of pegs hung with orange plastic bags, which are great for small toys like bricks, cars, and marbles. If you can make a game of putting things away, it won't seem such a chore.

It is also worth buying or building a cupboard with deep shelves and a set of transparent plastic crates. Label each crate with the name of an article of clothing, using a picture and the word,

so that there is no confusion and everything stays in its own crate. Hooks on the back of the door or along the chair rail as shown in the project should take care of most things that you need to hang up. Child-size wardrobes are also a good idea if you have a daughter with dresses—if the wardrobe is adult size, then fit an extra rail lower down for her to reach, and the top rail can be used for out-of-season clothes.

When we have children we often spend a great deal of time organizing their activities, lessons, and social events. It doesn't have to be this way all the time, though, and they also need to relax. Large floor cushions, beanbag chairs, or a small sofa-bed will also encourage them to think of the room as a place to snuggle down and think, read, and listen to stories.

A bed with storage space underneath is a good way of saving floor space. If the storage will be on show, like this bedroom, a matching set of brightly colored boxes will look fun.

THE PROJECTS

The projects on the following pages are a mixture of fun and function. Make sure you take your children's own preferences into account.

PROJECT ONE

Lining the walls with tongue-and-groove paneling

Wood paneling gives a very cosy, country feel to a room, and the peg rail on the pages 136–137 is such a useful addition that you will wonder how you ever managed without it. If you buy the tongue-and-groove paneling in kit form, it will be pre-cut and ready to fix to the wall. If you cut the lengths yourself, you may like to make it slightly lower than usual, which has

the effect of scaling down the room to the child's size. If you are impatient for the boarded effect, you can buy large panels of MDF that have been carved to give the effect of joined boards. They can simply be stuck to the wall using panel adhesive, although do bear in mind that removing them at a later date could affect the condition of the wall surface.

Tongue-and-groove paneling gives a children's room a cosy feel. The paneling can be bought in kit form and painted in your choice of colors. The "hockey-stick" molding on the top makes a useful shelf, or for a wider shelf and row of pegs, see pages 136–137.

HOW TO DO IT

STEP 1 Using the rule with the spirit level, mark three positions for the battening on the wall to align with the top, middle, and bottom of the panels.

STEP 2 Drill and insert wall anchors every 20 in. and then screw the battens onto the wall.

STEP 3 Beginning in one corner, place the end plank against the wall and check the vertical with the spirit level. Hammer a brad through the inside edge of the tongue, angled slightly inward. Do this into all three battens. Use the center punch with the hammer to drive the brad head below the surface.

STEP 4 Fit the groove of each subsequent plank into the tongue of the first. To ensure a tight fit, place a spare piece of wood along the edge, and tap it with the hammer to prevent damage to the plank's tongue. Continue in the same way to complete the paneling.

STEP 5 Fit a narrow batten along the top edge of the paneling using brads and a center punch.

STEP 6 Replace the baseboard, and then prime and paint the paneling in the color of your choice. If you are also fitting the rail and shelf, continue as explained in the steps overleaf, fitting the rail along the top of the paneling. If not, you will need to finish off the top of the panels with a square molding. This can be screwed into the wall or stuck on with panel adhesive.

- 3 x 1-IN. DAR SOFTWOOD TO FIT AROUND THE ROOM (MEASURE THE LENGTH REQUIRED)
- SHELF (THE SAME AMOUNT OF DAR SOFTWOOD AGAIN)
- SUPPORT BRACKETS FOR SHELF TO MATCH 3 IN. DEPTH OF SHELF
- PEGS (EITHER BUY TURNED PEGS OR MAKE THEM FROM A LENGTH OF DOWEL. DECIDE HOW MANY YOU NEED FOR NOW, MORE CAN ALWAYS BE ADDED LATER)
- LONG RULE WITH SPIRIT LEVEL
- PENCIL
- DRILL
- $5/16$-IN. BIT FOR CLEARANCE HOLES
- $1/4$-IN. BIT FOR WALL
- SPADE BIT FOR PEGS
- $1/4$-IN. WALL ANCHORS SUITABLE FOR YOUR KIND OF WALL
- PENCIL

PROJECT TWO

Fitting a peg rail and shelf

This can either be a continuation of the tongue-and-groove paneling project on the previous pages (pages 134–135), or a project on its own. If you decide against the paneling, you may not want to fit the peg rail and shelf on more than one wall. The instructions allow for this, and explain the order and technique, rather than giving exact measurements.

A row of pegs can make clearing-up fun. Hang a row of brightly colored bags on the pegs to hold small toys like bricks, cars, or marbles, or hang the toys directly on the pegs themselves. The shelf above offers even more storage space.

HOW TO DO IT

STEP 1 Cut the peg rail plank to fit the wall lengths, mitering the ends for a neat fit in the corners and at any joins. Check and mark the rail position on the wall with a spirit level. Drill clearance holes in the planks then mark, drill, and plug the wall, and screw the peg rail in place.

STEP 2 Use the spade bit to drill holes for the pegs, and then apply wood glue to their ends before pushing them firmly into the rail. If the pegs are to be painted different colors, it may be easier to do this before you fit them.

STEP 3 If you are adding a shelf to the top of the peg rail, do so now. Screw the peg rail to the wall.

STEP 4 Screw the shelf to the peg rail and through into the wall batten. Prime and paint.

YOU WILL NEED:
- **WHITE WOOD PRIMER**
- **2 BRIGHT-COLORED TEST POTS OF LATEX PLUS CLEAR VARNISH, OR 2 SEMIGLOSS OR EGGSHELL COLORS**
- **WATER-BASE BLACKBOARD PAINT**
- **SMALL FOAM ROLLER AND TRAY**
- **PAINT BRUSHES**
- **SANDPAPER**

PROJECT THREE

Painting MDF furniture and using blackboard paint

An ideal project to encourage your children's writing skills (or at least their noughts and crosses!) This is a small painting project that will make a big difference. Incorporate your children's two favorite colors to make it personal. You could apply the idea to any piece of furniture you already own, find a secondhand piece to make over, or buy an unpainted MDF blank. Blanks are nicely designed pieces of furniture made especially for people who enjoy applying the paint themselves. They are sold by mail order, and the money saved by not painting them is reflected in the price. You will find an address in the directory at the back of the book.

HOW TO DO IT

STEP 1 Sand the old paint to create a good surface for the paint to key into.

STEP 2 Prime the whole unit using a white water-based paint.

STEP 3 If the furniture has panels, paint as shown. If not, draw a square shape across the front and edge it with painter's tape.

STEP 4 Apply two coats of blackboard paint, and wait until dry before removing the tape.

PROJECT FOUR

Making photocopied fun cushions

T-shirt printing is available at most photocopying stores, and any image not protected by copyright laws can be photocopied onto a special film and transferred onto fabric. The image could be a photograph of your dog, a holiday snap, or an original drawing, cut-out, or pattern. Take a plain white square of cotton fabric to the photocopying store and ask them to transfer the image on to the fabric, then take it home and make up a cushion. The transfer film can also be bought for home use with a computer scanner and printer.

HOW TO DO IT

STEP 1 Cut out a square of white cotton fabric measuring roughly 16 x 16 in. Choose an image to be photocopied and trim it to a square shape.

STEP 2 Mark the size and position for the print on the white cotton fabric, and take this to the photocopiers. Ask them to enlarge and print the image onto your fabric.

STEP 3 Fold back a small hem on the printed fabric and pin it to the front of the cushion cover. Slipstitch by hand, or machine stitch.

Fantasy bedroom

Parents often find that having a young child gives them the opportunity to rediscover their artistic side, which may have been neglected since they left school. It's fantastic when you realize that the time has come to put all those skills learned in woodwork, art, and design lessons to good use.

A lot of the most exciting decorating programs on TV create rooms that are a mixture of window-dressing and stage design adapted for the home. Children's bedrooms can be treated in the same way, and all you need are basic skills, time, and imagination. There is no reason why their beds have to look like beds—so long as they are safe and comfortable to sleep in, they can be anything from caves to castles. The same approach can be used to transform the whole room into a complete fantasy world.

Children's bedrooms are often also their playrooms, so fun is a number one priority. But apart from safety and comfort, there are no rules when it comes to decorating children's rooms, so let your imagination run wild!

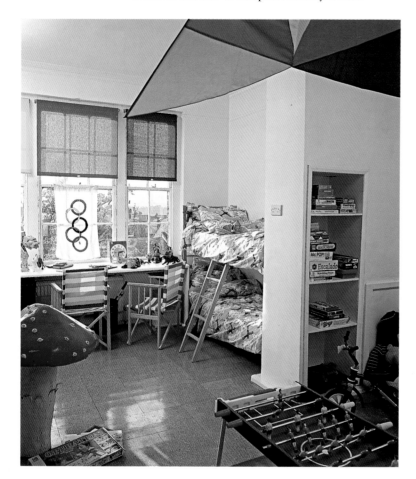

MDF beds

Children's beds can be expensive, but why buy one when you can make a very special one from MDF? The design chosen for the project on the following pages is a castle, and whether you have a little sleeping beauty or knight in shining armor, the bed is sure to be a hit.

The one very good reason why MDF is so popular is that it has no grain. When you work with natural wood, the direction of the grain is extremely important, particularly when cutting and planing. The main reason for this is that wood splits along the grain and if, for instance, you insert a row of screws in a line along the grain, the wood is very likely to split. Softwood is most prone to splitting because it is harvested from fast-growing trees, so the grain is less dense than with hardwood, which comes from slow-growing trees.

MDF is short for medium-density fiberboard. It is made from small, even-sized particles of wood that have been mixed with a chemical compound to bind them together before being compacted into sheets. You should always wear a mask when sawing through MDF, because the dust contains those binding chemical compounds, which can be harmful, and it is best not to do the cutting work in your child's bedroom, where the fine dust will be difficult to clear away completely. Once MDF is cut out and painted, it presents no greater health risk than any other construction material. The good news is that MDF can be cut into all kinds of shapes with a jigsaw. A bed like a castle is easy!

The castle theme

Once you have made the bed, turn your attention to other areas in the room to extend the castle theme. If you have shelving, it can be edged with strips cut out in the shape of battlements, and the bedcover could be decorated with appliqué shields or knight's heraldic flags. Curtain poles can have arrow-head finials (securely screwed to the wall!), and the toy chest could be made to look like a king's treasure chest.

If you are making the castle for a princess, she will probably also like the idea of a climbing rose winding its way up the battlements, with a

THE PROJECTS
The projects on the following pages show how to make and paint a castle bed. Some battlement shelving, a heraldic bedcover, and a king's treasure chest will complete the castle theme.

Role play is a favorite children's activity, so if their bedroom is designed like a stage, with a number of different scenes and settings, they'll be in heaven!

painted crown about her pillow and a silky bedcover to sleep under. Think of Queen Guinevere in Camelot, where ladies were wrapped in velvet trimmed with lace. If she is more of a Joan of Arc, it might be wiser to stick to battlements and suits of armor!

PROJECT ONE

The castle bed

The plan for the castle bed tells you what you need and exactly how it is made. This is the first stage of the project, and in the next stage there are ideas for how it can be painted. If you are keen to make a bed but not so keen on the castle idea, then the plan could be adapted. You could use the same basic construction method, but change the cut-out shape to give the bed a different theme. Cars and engines are always popular with boys. If your child has a favorite story or cartoon film, then that would be a good place to look for inspiration.

MDF is a perfect material for cutting out a castle's battlements. You could choose a different kind of building if you're not so keen on the castle idea.

HOW TO DO IT

This makes a bed that will fit a standard 32-in.-wide mattress.

STEP 1 Support the MDF between two saw horses or tables, and draw the cut-outs on the ends and the sides. Draw positional guidelines on the sides for the legs and the side battens. Use the long rule to draw them as continuous pencil lines.

STEP 2 Drill holes in the corners of each of the cut-outs to access the saw blade.

STEP 3 Wear a mask! Use the jigsaw carefully to cut out the shapes, then use sandpaper to round off the edges, paying particular attention to the sides of the bed, where the child will be climbing in and out.

STEP 4 Drill the pilot holes and countersink holes for the screws.

STEP 5 Glue and screw the legs and side battens in place.

STEP 6 Draw positional guides on the two ends for the legs, and to mark where the bed ends meet the sides on the MDF. Drill pilot holes and countersink the screws.

STEP 7 Drill, glue, and screw the MDF panels to the legs of the bed.

STEP 8 Glue and screw the ends to the sides.

STEP 9 Space out the base slats (mattress supports) and then drill pilot holes, and glue and screw them to the bed. Fill all the countersink holes and sandpaper smooth once the filler has set.

Follow these guidelines when you are making up your castle bed. Remember to measure everything properly, and use a spirit level to check that everything is level.

You will need:
- FOAM OFFCUTS ROUGHLY 2-IN. SQUARE
- PLATE
- SMALL FOAM ROLLER AND TRAY
- LATEX PAINT IN DARK AND LIGHT GREY
- CLEAR MATTE VARNISH

PROJECT TWO

Painting the castle bed

The method described here is just one way to paint the castle bed. You may prefer to paint it freehand, or all in one color (see page 142). This method shows a quick and easy way of giving the castle bed the appearance of weathered brickwork. You could use this method with another pale color, such as light blue.

HOW TO DO IT

STEP 1 Cut three or four foam squares into rough stone shapes. They can vary in size and be rounded off at the corners.

STEP 2 Use the foam roller to paint the whole bed in a base coat of light grey.

STEP 3 Thin the darker paint with water, 2 parts paint to 1 part water, then use the foam blocks to build up the castle brickwork. Cover with a coat of clear varnish when dry.

Nursery

When it comes to preparing for a new arrival, our instincts are like any animal's. We want to make a cozy nest and have everything ready for the big day. Nature is a wonderful thing, and even if you have never looked twice at a frieze of fluffy bunnies or frolicking lambs before, you will find the choice is suddenly a major one! A baby opens up a whole new world, and it's amazing that something so small needs that much stuff. In truth they don't, but we do, and as long so we keep spending, manufacturers will keep coming up with new ideas to make life with a baby easier and more pleasant.

These flimsy curtains may look nice, but they will make it impossible to encourage a baby to sleep in the daylight.

Decorating a nursery for a first baby is one of life's luxuries. The baby won't mind how you decorate it, but it gives expectant parents something positive to do, and there are lots of things to look out for.

Colors

If you already know the sex of your baby, you may want to follow a traditional pink or blue color scheme, or the usual alternative, which has always been pale yellow. One good reason for sticking to these colors is that they are the colors of most products, presents, and accessories for babies. Strong primary colors like red, yellow, and blue are great for later on, but they seem very harsh for a nursery. There are more gentle contemporary colors if you wish to avoid the pinks and blues, such as moss green, pale sea green, lavender, apricot, and buttery cream.

It may be difficult to imagine, but your baby will soon be a rampaging toddler and it is worth keeping this in mind when you decorate. Try to choose colors and styles that will either be appropriate later on, or that can be added to or adapted for a growing child.

Windows

The most important thing you need to know about nursery windows is that they need to have curtains or blinds that block out the light completely. This can be done by lining curtains with black or navy fabric, or using special blackout lining fabric. Flimsy muslin curtains will do nothing to convince a baby that it's time to sleep if the sun is still shining outside!

Roller blinds are fine for babies before they begin to investigate the way things work, but can be something of a hazard later on, when the pulls are grabbed too hard or suddenly let go of so that they shoot out of reach. Roman blinds fold up and down and are a better bet, because they don't need stiffening, can be lined with black-out, and are surprisingly easy to make.

Changing

Babies generate an incredible amount of washing, and you will need one or two laundry bins. Two will enable you to sort out the more urgent toweling hot wash from the rest when you change your baby. Changing diapers and baby clothes can be a backbreaking task if you are constantly leaning over, and it will be a lot easier if you have a changing table with everything you need close at hand. Baby clothes can be kept handy in drawers or baskets below, with cotton wool, wipes, and diapers all being within easy reach on the table top.

Sitting

In the early months it is a good idea to have a comfortable chair to sit in while you're feeding the baby. Have a small table with a lamp to read by as well, because you may want to consult any baby books you may have, or just need somewhere safe to put a drink down. Once your baby begins to crawl and climb up, everything that could topple over, like a small table with a lamp, should be removed from the room to prevent accidents.

Lighting

Central lights are the best and safest option in the nursery. Look out for a fabulous lampshade that will give your baby something to gaze at. Safe nightlights made specially for a child's room

can also be great fun, especially the ones that turn round and project images on the walls—babies love them.

Sleeping

Deciding whether to buy a crib or a cot is a personal choice. A cot is more practical because it will last for about three years, though tiny babies do look lost in them, but a crib is so sweet, and it is almost impossible to wear one out. Full-size cots are adjustable to three different heights. If you decide to use one from the start, have it at the highest level to avoid too much bending, and move it down as soon as your baby starts pulling up on the bars.

Pinks and blues are the colors of most baby products, presents, and accessories, so it makes sense to use these colors for walls.

Painting a gingham wall

YOU WILL NEED:

- SMALL FOAM ROLLER AND TRAY
- PAINTER'S TAPE ¹⁵/₈ IN. WIDE
- CRAFT OR SNAP-BLADE KNIFE
- WALLPAPER PASTE
- SPIRIT LEVEL
- PLUMB LINE (OPTIONAL)
- TEST POT OF PALE GREEN PAINT

Gingham is one of the freshest fabrics around, and it will never, ever go out of fashion. This project shows how to customize a small foam roller and give the nursery walls a gingham effect. You can do this on a colored background if you prefer, but white is traditional and always makes a room look bigger and brighter. Most nursery borders look good with gingham, and if you buy one first you can co-ordinate the colors.

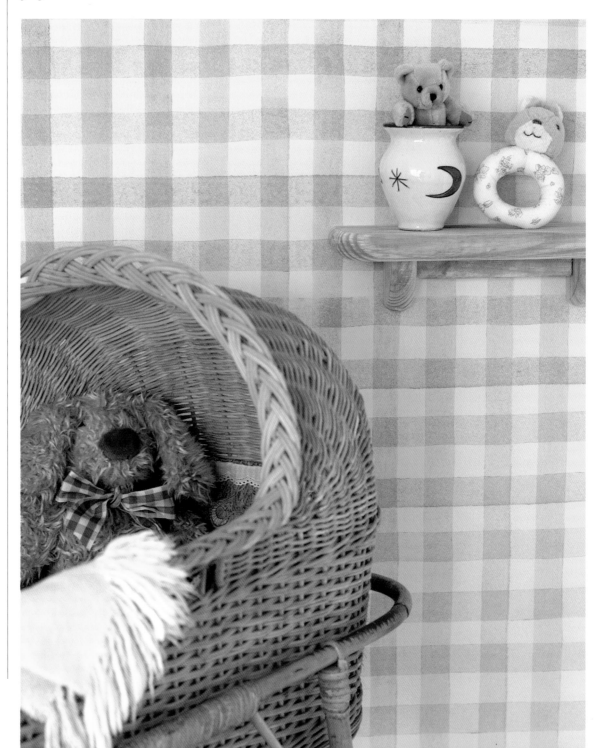

Gingham made easy—a simple trick with a small foam roller can transform a nursery wall, making it look bigger and brighter.

HOW TO DO IT

STEP 1 Wrap the painter's tape around the middle of the roller, dividing it into three equal parts.

STEP 2 Cut down to the middle of the roller in a straight line, following the edge of the tape. Turn the roller and cut all the way around, then once across between the lines.

STEP 3 Peel off the middle foam section, then peel off the painter's tape.

STEP 4 Mix the wallpaper paste following the instructions on the pack, and then mix it half and half with the paint in the roller tray.

STEP 5 Hang the plumb line from the top of the wall to give you a vertical guide to follow. Run the roller through the paint/wallpaper paste mixture and begin painting in one corner, applying a medium pressure and continuing to within about 2 in. of the baseboard. This final bit can be applied filled in with the offcut from the roller. Continue in this way to complete all the vertical stripes

STEP 6 Place the spirit level on the wall and make some small guide marks for the first horizontal band of striping. The next stripes can be aligned with the first, but check with the level on each alternate row so that you don't drift away from the horizontal.

PROJECT TWO

Making a removable changing table top

The first few months with a new baby can be very tiring, and it is impossible to imagine how backbreaking diaper changing can be if you are constantly bending over. This project shows you can make a table top which can sit on a chest of drawers, a small desk, or even a single kitchen unit at the right height, to make diaper changing a thousand times easier. It has been designed to be used lengthwise, with the back pushed up against the wall, and the supporting chest of drawers or desk pulled forward so that the front is level with the edge of the unit. Any foam-padded, sponge-cleanable changing mat will fit into the wooden frame. The exact dimensions will depend upon the size of the piece of furniture you are using as a base.

A portable table top for diaper changing makes the task far less backbreaking. Decide which piece of furniture you will use underneath before working out the dimensions.

HOW TO DO IT

STEP 1 Mark the base position on the back board and mark, screw, drill, and countersink the screws.

STEP 2 Place the top on your base in line with the front, and draw a line to mark the back edge.

STEP 3 Draw location guides on the base for the sides and the back. Drill pilot and countersunk holes for the screws.

STEP 5 Sandpaper all the edges to round them off, and then prime and paint the unit.

STEP 4 Cut the rounded corners on the front of both sides with a jigsaw. Glue and screw the back to the base from below, followed by both sides. Fill the screw holes with filler.

YOU WILL NEED:
- FISHING LINE
- 44-IN. LENGTH OF STRAIGHT WIRE
- 2 8-IN. LENGTHS OF STRAIGHT WIRE
- SCRAP OF STIFF CARD
- SCISSORS
- BALL-POINT PEN
- COLORED FELT
- COTTON BATTING
- NEEDLE AND THREAD
- GLUE
- SEQUINS AND SMALL BLACK BUTTONS FOR EYES
- HOOK FOR HANGING

PROJECT THREE

Fish mobile

There is one other essential ingredient to keep a baby happy in the nursery, and that is a mobile. It is made from simple felt shapes hung from three mobile wires on nylon thread. Make sure that the mobile is always well out of the baby's reach.

This colorful fish mobile, made out of simple felt shapes, should provide a welcome distraction for a baby in his or her cot.

HOW TO DO IT

STEP 1 Draw a fish shape onto a piece of card and cut it out. Use this as a template to draw 10 fish shapes on the felt.

STEP 2 Cut out the fish and put them together in pairs. Sew around the outside, leaving a small gap for the stuffing. Stuff each fish with a small amount of cotton batting, and slipstitch the gap closed. Glue the sequins onto the middle of the fish as scales. Sew two small buttons on each one for eyes.

STEP 3 Cut one length of fishing line to hang the mobile at the correct height. Then cut 4 x 12-in. lengths, 2 x 8-in. lengths and 2 x 6-in. lengths.

STEP 4 Twist the wires over at both ends to make loops. Thread the fishing line onto a needle and attach a line to each fish (as shown). Tie the lines onto the wires (as shown). Screw a hook to the ceiling and hang the fishy mobile over the cot or changing area.

Bathrooms

Today's bathrooms are more than simply a place to wash. They have become sanctuaries for pampering and indulgence, a tranquil retreat in which to relax and unwind, a beauty salon in your own home. As one of the first rooms you see in the morning, and one of the last you see at night, it's no wonder a bathroom's decor and style can make such a difference to how you start or end the day. This section shows how to transform your bathroom into one of two different styles, Traditional or Contemporary, before looking specifically at the shower room. Choose a style, choose a project, and go full steam ahead!

Traditional bathroom

The bathrooms that we now tend to think of as being traditional are actually early 20th-century in style, when the bathroom first became a feature in ordinary people's houses. Modern people were a bit slow on the uptake as far as bathrooms went, but the Romans had stunning baths and flushing toilets long ago. There was a gap until the first bath was installed in the White House in 1851, and there was no bathroom in Buckingham Palace when Queen Victoria began her reign in 1837. By the end of it, though, all kinds of bathroom fixtures had been invented, including stand-up showers, short and long bathtubs, flushing toilets, mixer faucets, and heated towel rails. And now there has never been more choice in bathroom fittings and fixtures, so whatever your idea of traditional may be, you can satisfy every whim.

A freestanding bathtub positioned in the center of the room with an old-style shower above looks wonderful. If you're buying an old iron bathtub, check your floor joists are strong enough to support it first.

With such a huge choice of bathroom fittings and fixtures, it's a good idea to make a list of the things you would like in your traditional bathroom before you begin redecorating. Nine things to consider are…

Planning

If you are planning a complete bathroom refit, then this is a good opportunity to move things around. Just because the bathtub is against one wall doesn't mean that that is the only place for it. The bathroom may have been planned by someone with no imagination or design skills, and now is your big chance to give it a complete new look. The best way to begin is to visit a bathroom showroom—the most upmarket one you can find—and pick up all the latest catalogs. Always start by looking at the best designs and work backward to something that suits your budget. That way you will immediately be able to spot the best features in the cheaper range, and see where savings can be made without any loss of style.

Some bathroom catalogs include a planning section, but if not you can make one yourself, using graph paper and scaled down cut-outs of the main fixtures. Mark the position of the window

and door on your plan, and then see if the bathtub, basin, or toilet are in the best places. If the door takes up space when open, perhaps it could be re-hung to open outward or even be moved further along the wall. Pipes and the electricity supply can always be re-routed if a new arrangement makes more sense. And if you have a large bathroom, the bathtub could be moved away from the wall into the middle of the room. Plan the lighting at the beginning of the project, and make the most of any natural light by painting the window frames white and fitting blinds into the frame recess. If you have a window with a view that is not overlooked, position the bath so that you can enjoy the view when you're in it. Mirrors should be placed in both useful and flattering positions!

Old v New Fixtures and Fittings

If you choose a period-style bathroom suite, you can opt for the real thing or a reproduction version. Many companies make reconditioned bathtubs and basins, or you could visit an architectural salvage yard, which is great fun and usually has lower prices than antique stores. Before buying an old iron bathtub you must find out whether your bathroom floor joists are strong enough to support its weight

Original wooden floorboards look lovely in a traditional bathroom, either stripped and painted with a waterproof floor paint, or simply stripped and varnished.

plus 242 lb. of water plus a person! Old faucets may look wonderful, but might not have the right-size pipe connectors for modern plumbing, so do find out what it will cost to have them updated before celebrating your bargain buy. Since most old styles of fixtures and fittings have been copied, it is often best to buy the new versions and attach them to the bathtub. Old lace shelf-edgings, glass bottles, mirror frames, and shelves add to the atmosphere without costing a fortune. And treat yourself, at least once, to expensive bottled bath products to display on the shelves—you can always refill them with the supermarket version later on!

Showers

A separate shower room is ideal, and it does not have to be much bigger than the average cubicle, but for most people a shower has to be fitted into the bathroom, either as a self-contained unit or over the bathtub. There are lots of options, and it is best to get advice from an expert. Begin by asking a plumber which system is best suited to your home. It will depend upon several factors,

including the siting of your cold water tank, the water pressure, and your boiler type. Armed with this information, you will be able to pass on the technical details to the sales staff, and confine your efforts to your favorite style. If you are fitting a power shower unit over a bath, then a shower curtain will not be enough to protect the surroundings, and you will need to have a panel or folding screen, which can be quite costly.

Electricity

Never be tempted to do a DIY electrical job in the bathroom. Wait until you've got a few jobs that need doing, and then employ a qualified electrician to install new fittings and check old ones at the same time. By law all switches have to be outside the bathroom, and an electrician will make sure that all the correct procedures are followed.

Lighting

Bathroom light fittings must have suitable sealed units for safety reasons. All switches must be pull-cords, and all fittings must be kept well clear of any potential splashes. The lighting should create a relaxing atmosphere with efficient illumination where it is most needed.

Walls

Steamy bathrooms need walls with water-resistant surfaces, which is why glazed tiles are so practical around basins, toilets, and bathtubs. The damp that often occurs in bathrooms happens when they are not very well ventilated in winter and condensation becomes a problem.

Wood paneling is an old idea, but for those not keen on tiling it is the most popular choice. The paneling can be laid over existing tiles to save work in removing them.

You can buy special paints for bathrooms made with added fungicides to combat mold, but if you don't want to introduce such chemicals into the atmosphere, then stick to an oil-based eggshell or latex paint, or a latex sealed with waterproof varnish.

One of the projects in this section shows how to line a bathroom with tongue and groove paneling. Although it is an old idea, it has now become the most popular alternative to tiling. It is not necessary to remove old tiles when you change to paneling, or indeed when you change tiles, as the new ones can simply be laid over the existing ones. If you are re-tiling, do it in a brickwork pattern to give the tiles a brand new look. If you want to refresh the tiling on a tight budget, use tile paint to change the color, or simply re-grout the existing tiles to give them a fresh new look.

Floors

Bathroom floors get wetter than any other floor in the home, especially if you have young children, and there is no doubt that non-slip, sheet vinyl is the best option. This can be sealed along the edges with silicone so that no water can seep underneath. The range of patterns and prices is huge, and there will be something to suit all tastes and budgets. Small bathrooms could be tackled with off-cuts, so get measuring before you visit a showroom and ask if they have a selection of roll ends. Your choice will certainly be limited to what is available, but do have a look. If you prefer carpets, choose one with a rot-proof latex backing, and use a bathmat with waterproof backing as well. Floating wooden floors are not suitable for bathrooms, but original wooden floorboards look lovely stripped and varnished, or painted with a waterproof floor paint. A stenciled pattern or different shades or colors for the border creates further interest.

Storage

All your hard work will be wasted if the bathroom shelves and bathtub surround become cluttered with shampoo bottles, razors, and toothbrushes. Assess your space and make the most of any dead areas for storage. They include wall-to-ceiling space above the toilet, above the end of the bathtub, and the wall under the sink. If extra towels are to be kept in the bathroom, they can be folded and put on display.

Essential luxury

A bathroom is a room for self-indulgence, somewhere to relax and recharge your batteries. It is a room to indulge in small luxuries, and they should be included in the budget. Scented candles, bubble bath, a large fluffy towel on a heated rail, and the right bath mat can make you feel as pampered as any supermodel. Remember that everything in the bathroom does not have to have hard edges and, if you can, find room for an upholstered chair to help create a relaxed atmosphere.

THE PROJECTS

The four projects on the following pages will help achieve a traditional background in your bathroom. Some period-style fixtures and fittings, and a big pile of fluffy towels should do the rest.

Cupboards can help hide cleaning materials, spare toilet rolls, and toiletry clutter in your bathroom. Look for some dead space in the bathroom where you could fit a small freestanding or wall-mounted unit.

YOU WILL NEED:

MATERIALS

• TONGUE AND GROOVE
  PANELING TO FIT
  AROUND THE WALLS.
  (MEASURE AND BUY
  PANELING KITS TO FIT
  THE LENGTH
  REQUIRED)
• THREE LENGTHS OF
  1 x ½-IN. BATTENS
  FOR EACH WALL
  LENGTH
• SHELF 3 x 1-IN. DAR
  SOFTWOOD TO FIT
  AROUND THE ROOM
  (MEASURE THE
  LENGTH REQUIRED)
• SUPPORT BRACKETS
  FOR THE SHELF, TO BE
  SPACED 24 IN. APART
• ¼-IN. WALL
  ANCHORS
• BOX OF NO. 6
  2-IN. SCREWS
• BOX OF 1-IN. BRADS
• SMALL HAMMER
• DRILL WITH ¼-IN.
  AND 3⁄32-IN. PILOT
  BITS
• FINE CENTER PUNCH
• MITER SAW OR BLOCK
  WITH BACKSAW
• SCREWDRIVER
• LONG RULE WITH
  SPIRIT LEVEL
• PENCIL

PROJECT ONE

Lining the walls with tongue-and-groove paneling

This is a lovely style for a bathroom that can be given a country or seaside accent, depending upon the color and paint finish used. You may even like the idea of staining the wood dark brown to give it a distinctly masculine style. The shelf around the top of the paneling can have hooks screwed into it for hanging up small hand towels and flannels.

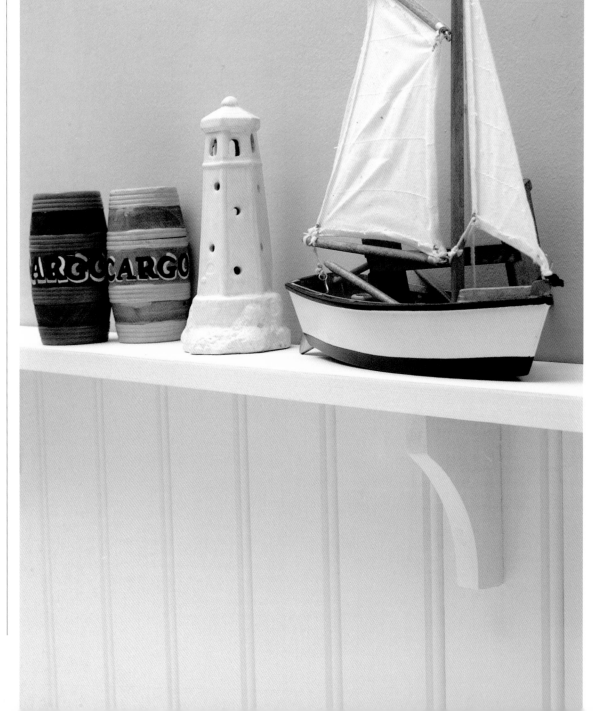

Wooden paneling can be customized to the style you want by the choice of paint color—blues and greens for a seaside theme, or earthy browns and creams for a country feel. Dark-brown wood stain will give it a masculine style.

HOW TO DO IT

STEP 1 Use the rule with the spirit level to mark three positions for the battening on the wall to align with the top, middle, and bottom of the panels. Drill and insert wall anchors spaced 20 in. apart, and then screw the battens onto the wall.

STEP 2 Beginning in one corner, place the end plank against the wall and check the vertical with the spirit level. Hammer a brad through the inside edge of the tongue angled slightly inward. Do this into all three battens. Use the center punch with the hammer to drive the brad head below the surface.

STEP 3 Fit the groove of the next plank into the tongue of the first. To ensure a tight fit, place a spare piece of wood along the edge and tap it with the hammer. Continue in the same way to complete the paneling. Planks will almost certainly need to be cut down to fit at the corners. Draw a line where this is required, clamp the plank in the jaws of a workbench, and cut with a backsaw or power saw.

STEP 4 Use a center punch to knock the brad heads into the lumber.

STEP 5 Cut the shelf planks to fit the wall lengths, mitering the ends for a neat fit in the corners and at any joins. Check and mark the shelf position on the wall with a spirit level. Drill pilot holes in the planks and the panels for the brackets.

STEP 6 Screw the brackets into the front of the paneling and down through the shelf into the top of the brackets. Prime and paint with enamel paint, or latex sealed with marine-quality varnish.

PROJECT TWO

Hanging a curtain below a basin

This project makes a pretty addition to a traditional bathroom, and also provides a concealed storage area below the basin for cleaning materials. Basins are made to many different designs, some rounded and others square at the front. Hardboard is used here to make a curved strip that fixes on to the wall behind the basin. The curtain is attached with strong Velcro, but for a quick fix you could use staples instead, and then cover the staples with a braid or ribbon held in place with strong glue. This will make it harder to remove and wash.

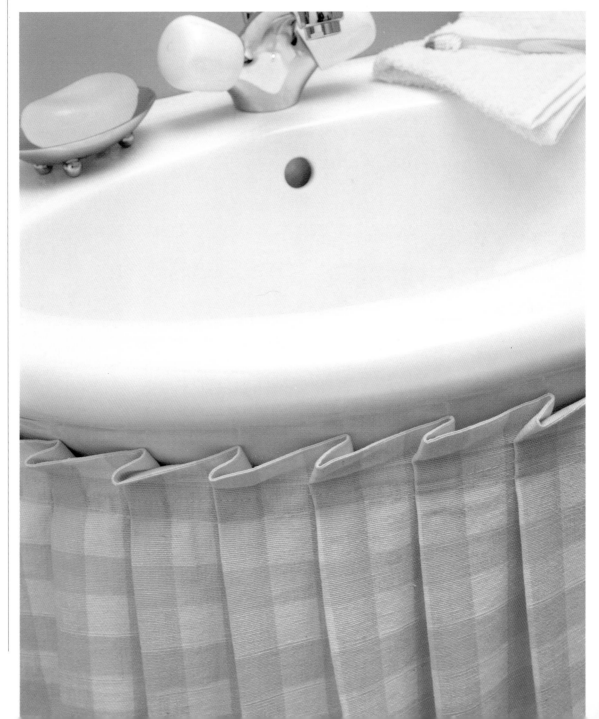

A simple curved strip of hardboard provides a curtain rail around a basin, creating extra storage space beneath the basin, as well as an attractive bathroom feature.

HOW TO DO IT

STEP 1 Mark the positions for the two wall battens just below the outside edge of the basin, using a rule and pencil.

STEP 2 Drill two holes to secure each batten and fit them with wall anchors. Screw the battens in position.

STEP 4 Attach the sticky side of the Velcro to the hardboard, and the other side to the curtains. Allow one to overlap the other by about 1 ⅛ in. in the front so that the curtains don't gape (or staple the fabric to the hardboard, and then glue on a braid or ribbon to cover the staples).

STEP 3 Dampen the hardboard to make it more flexible and then attach it, shiny side out, below the sink. Attach one side of the hardboard to the batten with the pins, then bend the hardboard into a curve and attach the other side to the other batten in the same way.

YOU WILL NEED:
• ABRASIVE POWDER
  AND CLOTH TO CLEAN
  THE BOARDS
• ELECTRIC SANDER,
  WITH COARSE GRADE
  SANDPAPER
• CENTER PUNCH
  AND HAMMER
• PRIMER
• THREE SHADES OF
  BLUE WOOD WASH
  OR LATEX PAINT
• PAINT BRUSHES
• MARINE-QUALITY
  CLEAR VARNISH
• SMALL ROLLER
  AND TRAY

PROJECT THREE

Painting floorboards

If you live in an old house, you will most likely have floorboards in the bathroom. A painted wooden floor looks nice, but a striped wooden floor is even better. The idea is to take one main color and two shades of it, one slightly deeper and one slightly lighter, giving an effect of subtle shading. Start painting at the far wall, and work back toward the door.

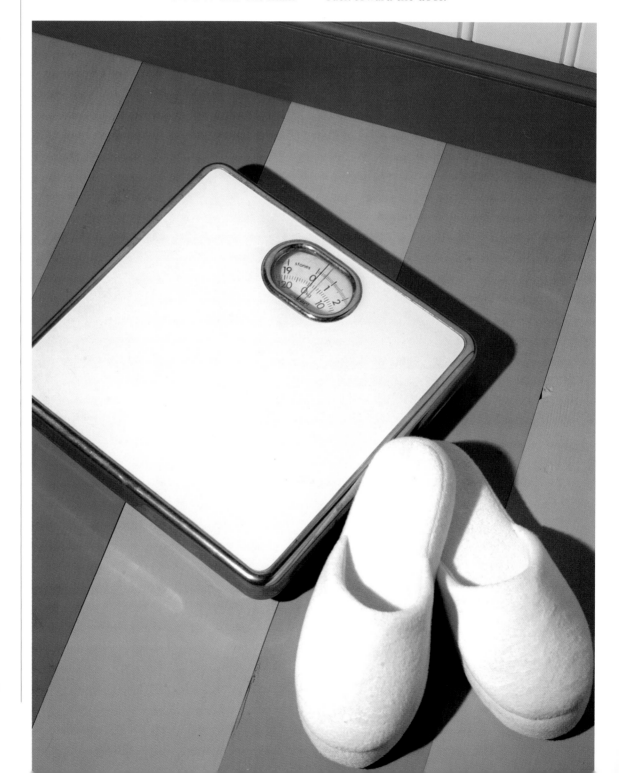

Original wooden floorboards look great painted in stripes contrasting three shades of the same color.

HOW TO DO IT

STEP 1 Sweep the floor and then check all the nails, firmly tapping down any that protrude using the center punch and a hammer.

STEP 2 Use the electric sander to get rid of any rough areas that could cause splinters. Don't spend too much time doing this, because the paint and varnish will add a smooth finish.

STEP 3 Scrub the floor with an abrasive powder solution and leave it to dry.

STEP 4 Begin painting, with the darker shade next to the far baseboard. Paint the next board in the main color (this is likely to be used elsewhere in the room).

STEP 5 Paint the third color and then repeat this sequence back across the room toward the door. It will be easier to paint the last three boards once the rest have dried, letting you reach into the corners and up to the baseboard.

STEP 6 Finally apply at least two coats of clear varnish, allowing the correct drying time between coats.

YOU WILL NEED:
- WINDOW CLEANER
- PAPER TOWEL
- THIN PAPER
- SCISSORS
- ADHESIVE SPRAY
- ETCHING SPRAY

PROJECT FOUR

Decorating a window with an etched pattern

If you have a small bathroom or very little natural light coming in, it is a shame to block the window with curtains or blinds. And when bathrooms are fitted with thick obscuring glass designed to stop the neighbors seeing you in the bath, this is not always very attractive. In both cases, and with plain glass, the window can be decorated with etching spray. This will allow you to keep clear glass in the top half of the window and stencil a frosted pattern of your own creation on the lower section, to give you all the privacy you need.

A window decorated with etching spray is a subtle and attractive way of creating privacy without blocking out the light with drapes or blinds.

HOW TO DO IT

STEP 1 Clean the window and let it dry. Fold four strips of paper 1 ⅛-in. wide and the length and height of the window into a concertina, then cut out a fancy pattern on one edge. Flatten the strips out and lightly apply adhesive spray to one side.

STEP 2 Fold another three strips of paper into 1 ⅛-in. squares concertina-wise, and draw simple motifs in the middle. Cut these out and spray one side lightly as above.

STEP 3 Stick the borders around the window up to the desired height, and then arrange the motifs across the window pane in a geometric or random pattern. Mask out the surrounding area with paper to protect it from the spray.

STEP 4 Spray on a light and even coating of etching spray. You can always apply a second coat if this is too thin and patchy, but it is best to apply one continuous coat first and then leave it to dry. Peel off one of the motifs to check the effect, and apply a second coat of etching spray if necessary.

Contemporary bathroom

Big changes have been taking place in the bathroom. It began in new hip hotels, where minimalism took over from opulence, and before long everyone was at it. This look is the antidote to Victorian and 19th-century repro style, which was the last big style statement for bathrooms. The big thing to note is that fashions take longer to change in bathrooms for the obvious reason that you can't move things around or replace them on a whim. The second factor is cost, because this is a room where expert help is definitely required, and plumbers, electricians, and builders don't come cheap. If you are going for a complete change, then it may be worth asking an architect or specialist bathroom designer to advise you.

The contemporary bathroom replaces opulence with minimalism, giving domestic bathrooms the hip hotel look.

Plumbers and electricians often work together on bathroom installations, and it is worth finding a pair who work well as a team. An electric shower, for instance, needs the expertise of a plumber and electrician at different stages. It is also a good idea to consult a plumber before you hire a designer, because you need to know what the water pressure is, the type of boiler, and size of tank. The plumber will also be able to advise you, for instance, whether it is worth replacing an old boiler at the same time to accommodate a shower system, which would be more economical to run. And if you can find a "new wave" creative plumber who keeps up with what's new in bathrooms, you won't be needing any other bathroom design advice.

Shop around

The first step is to get hold of as many top-class catalogs as you can and make your style choice. Cut out your favorites and prepare to move downmarket in search of lookalikes. As with clothes stores, there are lots of budget versions of the latest styles, and hardware outlets should be your first port of call. If you are on a tight budget, always go for the plainest designs, because they will be the slowest to date.

There is also a booming mail order trade in bathroom fixtures and fittings, and you may be able to economize by getting hold of a plain bathtub and toilet from a hardware store, making your style statement with accessories and a state-of-the-art sink. Bathroom cabinets, heated towel rails, mirrors, shelves, lights, and laundry baskets can all be bought in co-ordinating contemporary ranges, and extra items can go on a birthday or Christmas present list!

The best advice is to shop around before you buy, because some copies of designer items are as low on quality as they are on price, and it may be worth waiting for a sale of the real thing, or buying last year's range from an outlet. That is particularly true because style changes take a long time to filter down to the cheap end of the market, sometimes taking two or three years.

Planning a brand new bathroom

One of the most important aspects of planning is your budget, and it should include the cost of the main sanitaryware (bathtub, toilet, bidet, basin, shower tray), the faucets, shower, and the screen or cubicle. Also include decorating materials such as tiles, paint, flooring, and essential accessories like storage units, lights, towel rails, mirrors, and shelves. Get quotes for the plumbing, electrics, and carpentry, and any decorating that you can't manage yourself, such as skim coating or replastering. If you add these up and are still smiling, skip the next paragraph!

Upgrading your old bathroom

If you like the idea of a new bathroom but not the price, it's time to take stock and take action. If the bathroom suite is outdated or plain ugly, it will have to be disguised. Materials to think about are pure white laminated board, sheet acrylic, or sheet metal. If you like the look of an aluminum bathtub panel but not its price, then buy a sheet of marine ply and spray it with metallic aluminum spray paint. Spend money on the trim, and it will look every bit as good as the real thing. Paint is still the cheapest and most dramatic way to make changes, and you can use it on walls, tiles, woodwork, and even vinyl flooring.

Pick a color scheme with a contemporary feel, something like ice blue, linen white, and café latte with accents of dull silver. Box in the bathtub and basin with plywood, paint the walls ice blue and linen white, paint the floor café latte, and fit matching colored blinds. Then change the toilet seat, shower curtain, bath mat, toilet roll

PAINTING TILES AND FLOORS
In the 1990s, interior designers' quest for originality meant that products on the industrial side were taken up by the home sector. Non-slip floor paints were one of the first products to cross over from the factories and shipyards, and many other resurfacing products and specialized finishes followed. The next four projects show how to transform three shiny bathroom surfaces: tiles are primed and painted, vinyl flooring is given a whole new look, and a window is decorated with etching spray.

holder, towel rail, and mirror. This doesn't necessarily mean buy everything new—keep a look out for things that can be transformed with paint, like woven laundry baskets or mirror frames. Galvanized metal is very cheap and has been taken up by some contemporary designers for mirror frames, candle holders, and small cupboards. Classic items like buckets and utility shelving can be bought from hardware stores and integrated with designer buys. In short, this is the sort of quick fix that you can do in a weekend. So what on earth are you waiting for?

Designer catalogs can help you decide on the look you want, before looking for a budget version. Sometimes it's worth waiting for a sale of the real thing to prevent sacrificing quality for price.

YOU WILL NEED:

- ABRASIVE POWDER OR WALL AND FLOOR CLEANER
- SCOURING SPONGE
- OLD TOWEL
- TILE PRIMER
- SMALL FOAM ROLLER AND TRAY
- PAINTER'S TAPE
- ENAMEL OR EGGSHELL PAINT IN CHOSEN COLOR
- EXTRA ROLLER

PROJECT ONE

Painting tiles

This is one of those miracles where doing and seeing what you've done is believing.

NOTE

If you want the tiles to look convincingly ceramic, then scrape out the old grout before you paint and re-grout the tiles afterward, following the steps shown in the tile grouting project.

HOW TO DO IT

STEP 1 Wash down the tiled area, and dry it well with an old towel to get rid of any surface water. Mask off the edges of the tiled area with painter's tape, and then pour some of the tile primer into the tray and apply a thin, even coat with the small foam roller. Leave to dry. If the tile pattern or color shows through, then apply one more coat. Clean the tray and fit a new roller.

STEP 2 Pour the feature color paint into the tray and use the roller to apply it to the tiles. Leave to dry and then apply a second coat.

Old tiles can be transformed into ceramic lookalikes with a coat of tile primer and a coat of enamel.

YOU WILL NEED:

- VINYL FLOOR PAINT (3.7 GAL. COVERS 150 SQ. FT.)
- ABRASIVE POWDER
- LARGE SPONGE
- BUCKET
- SMALL, HIGH-DENSITY SPONGE ROLLER AND TRAY

Transform those hated vinyl floor patterns with a couple of coats of paint. Try to allow a few days for it to dry, to make it last longer.

PROJECT TWO

Painting a vinyl floor

This may seem like a very lazy option, but don't knock it if it works! Vinyl flooring is the most practical and comfortable flooring for a bathroom, but some of the patterns really let the material down. Until recently, the only options were to live with it or rip it out and fit new flooring, but there is now a third option, and that is paint. It is much cheaper and far less hassle to use than cutting out templates and replacing something that's practical, and in good condition, because you loathe the color or pattern. The paint is a specialist type, but it is now available from several major hardware outlets.

HOW TO DO IT

STEP 1 Before you begin painting, the floor must be spotlessly clean. Fill a bucket with hot water and dissolve the abrasive powder as directed. Clean the floor and leave it to dry.

STEP 2 Apply the paint with the roller. Do not apply it too thickly because it will develop an unpleasant film. If, however, you apply it too thinly it will wear off. For the best results, apply two to three even coats for a thorough covering. The first coat should be touch-dry in an hour and the second coat can be applied in 4 hours time. The paint can be walked on after 6 hours, but will be even tougher if you leave it for a few days. It will provide a long-lasting finish.

Colored grouting

Grout is the filler between tiles, which can be used decoratively to make a very obvious grid of colored lines. It comes in a good range of colors and is easy to apply.

YOU WILL NEED:
- COLORED GROUTING IN A COLOR OF YOUR CHOICE
- SCRAPER OR SMALL SCREWDRIVER TO CLEAN OUT OLD GROUT
- SPONGE WITH SCOURER
- FLEXIBLE GROUT SPREADER
- GROUT SHAPER (ROUND-ENDED)
- SOFT DRY CLOTH

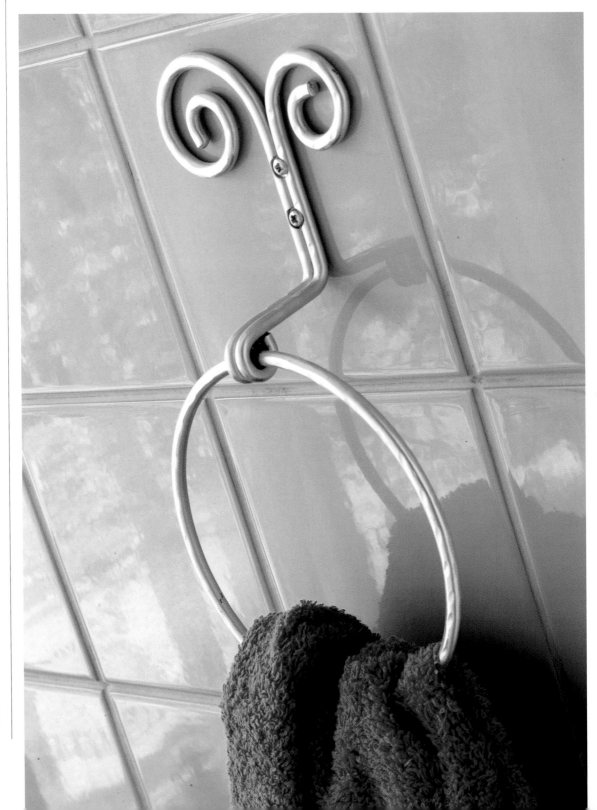

The finishing touches to freshly painted tiles, or simply to freshen up existing tiles, colored grouting is an easy way to give your tiles a new look.

HOW TO DO IT

STEP 1 Run the grout scraper (or another suitable tool) along the old grout and scrape most of it away. Don't allow the scraper to skid across the tiles and damage the surface, or to dig too deep and affect the tile adhesive.

STEP 2 Dampen the scouring sponge and run it down the scraped gaps between the tiles to remove any loose material.

STEP 3 Use a flexible spreader to press the grout into the gaps so that there are no air bubbles left.

STEP 4 Next, use the sponge to wipe away any excess grout from the tiles, and use a shaping tool to mold the grout into a slightly concave shape. Wipe away any smears, leave to dry, and finally polish the tiles with a dry, soft cloth.

YOU WILL NEED:

• DE-GREASING
  WINDOW CLEANING
  SPRAY AND CLOTH
• ETCHING SPRAY
• PAINTER'S TAPE
• TAPE MEASURE
  OR RULE
• PLAIN PAPER
• ADHESIVE SPRAY

PROJECT FOUR

Decorating a window with etching spray

This gives a cool, contemporary look to a bathroom window, and obscures the view from outside. The design is more of a style statement, and the spray could also be used to make a matching border for a bathroom mirror. The same spray is used for a project in the traditional bathroom, so just follow the steps for the method.

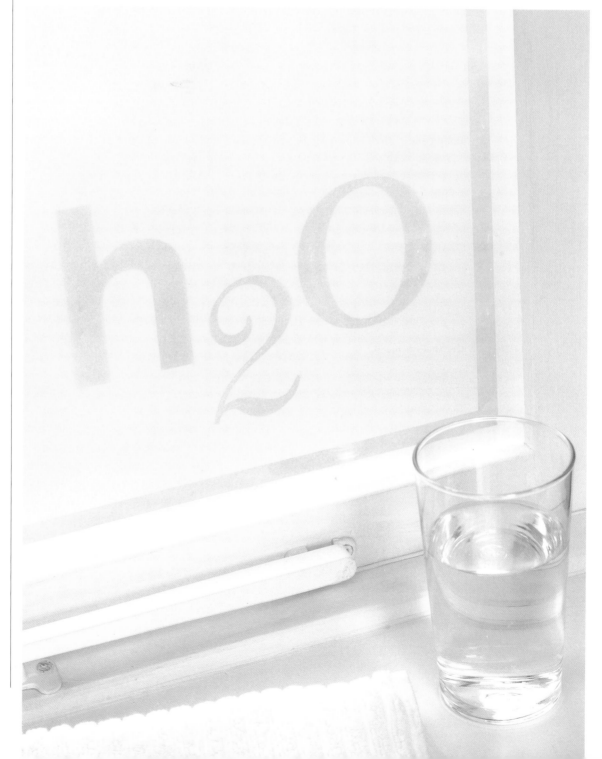

Decorating a window with etching spray gains privacy without curtains or blinds, while adding a cool, contemporary look. Your own design would do just as well as the one shown.

HOW TO DO IT

STEP 1 Run a frame of painter's tape ¾ in. inside the edge of the window, attaching paper to protect the surrounding area.

STEP 2 Enlarge the "h_2o" on a photocopier to fill an A4 sheet, then cut them out and apply adhesive spray to the back. Place the letters inside the masked frame and then frost the window with the etching spray. Peel off the tape and the templates.

Shower room
A home with a bathroom and separate shower room has the best of both worlds, allowing you to freshen up quickly, or relax and enjoy a long soak in warm bubbles. Ensuite bathrooms are often shower rooms through lack of space. But even if space is not an issue, if you really prefer a shower to a bath anytime, it could make sense to get rid of the bath altogether and enjoy the luxury of a spacious shower room instead. And if, at a later date, you decide you do want a bathtub, one can simply be put in.

You can now find showers small enough to fit into almost any space, so cupboards become potential shower rooms.

In a small apartment, a shower is more economical space-wise, and is also a good option as an en-suite facility for teenagers. This idea could save many a row over how long certain people spend in the bathroom! However, babies and very small children usually hate showers and getting water in their eyes, and washing their hair under an overhead shower can be a nightmare, so stick to the sink for that job. Or try an adjustable shower that you can set at the right height so you don't splash water in their faces, which is what tends to cause all the fuss.

A range of possibilities
If you are starting a shower room from scratch, it is worth considering doing without a cubicle and tray, and instead turning the whole room into a walk-in shower. You will need the help of a plumber, electrician, and carpenter. The shower fittings are fixed on the wall, and the floor will have to be raised slightly to create a slope to a central drain. The shower room can then be tiled, grouted, and silicone-sealed. Slatted wooden boards are also a good idea on part of the floor, to prevent slipping and minimize puddles. The luxury of a shower room like this could actually cost less than buying a new tray and cubicle.

If you are fitting a cubicle, tray, and shower in a small room that doesn't have a toilet or basin, try not to clutter it up too much, because space is one of the biggest luxuries in a shower room. Walls only need to be tiled outside the shower unit if it doesn't have glass on all sides, so the rest of the room can be decorated for comfort and convenience. Have a rail to warm towels over the radiator, or replace the radiator with a large, heated towel rail. A bathroom cupboard, shelf, and a mirror with good lighting are the other essentials. If the room is small and square, this might also be a good place to fit a false ceiling with recessed lights fitted with a dimmer switch, operated from outside the shower room. All lighting should be of the sealed-unit type suitable for bathrooms. And also make sure there is some ventilation, because steam needs to escape if you are to avoid condensation problems.

Adaptability
Shower manufacturers boast of making units that can fit into almost any space, and that can mean somewhere as small as a cupboard. And with new combination boilers, water is heated on demand without the need for a large hot-water storage tank in an airing cupboard. So if you are changing the boiler, why not investigate the possibility of fitting a new shower? Who knows, your airing cupboard may just be big enough for a shower with a folding door. Another good shower option is having one near the back door. This is especially useful if you live near the beach, on a farm, or

and applied in sheets, which makes tiling curves easier than you would imagine. Mosaics come in many other colors than "swimming pool" blue, and while you're at it, why not try your hand at a mirror frame or simple frieze? Be warned, though, the mosaic habit is a difficult one to kick. The best floor treatment for a shower room like this would be tiles or sheet vinyl, but do make sure that you always step onto a dry bath mat to avoid wet feet on the bedroom carpet.

If the ensuite is for a teenager, make sure that there are plenty of hooks to hang up towels, and a radiator to dry the bath mat on. One day they'll realize that towels and bath mats are revolting if they stay on the floor in a wet heap! It is also vital to make sure that the shower is totally watertight, and it may even be worth building a low tiled wall that you step over at the entrance to the room. It is better to anticipate problems now than deal with them later.

There is one element to showering that hasn't really been mentioned, and that is the pleasure to be had from standing under a powerful stream of warm water. A power shower option is a really good idea for those times when you need kick-starting in the morning, or when you need a blast to unwind you after work. Ask your plumber about a power-shower pump unit, which can be switched on and off from outside the bathroom. This will allow you to conserve hot water and electricity when an ordinary shower will do, and will give you the option of having an exhilarating power shower when you really need it.

have an occupation or play a sport that means you return home dirty and sweaty. It is also an ideal place for kids to be sluiced down as they come in from the garden. This is a no-frills sort of shower, with rendered and tiled wallboard, and a heavy-duty PVC shower curtain on a rail. Fit a mirror, and soap and shampoo tray inside, and have a handy towel hook outside with a wooden duckboard to step out onto.

Ensuite shower room

An ensuite shower room must be waterproof, warm, and welcoming. Privacy comes with the territory, and you can afford to think more about the design and less about the barricading. Flexible MDF is a relatively new material that makes building curves possible. This could be used to create the base for a curved mosaic wall instead of a glass shower cubicle. Mosaic tiles can be bought

(Left) Only the inside walls of a shower cubicle need tiling. The other walls can be decorated with paint.

A refreshing wake-up shower in an ensuite shower room is a perfect morning tonic, especially if you add the exhilaration of a power shower.

THE PROJECTS
The main issues facing you when decorating a shower room are what to do about the walls and floor. The following projects offer some ideas.

YOU WILL NEED:

- 8 x 2 3/4-IN. LENGTHS OF 2 x 1-IN. DAR PINE
- 2 x 1 3/4-IN. LENGTHS OF 2 x 1-IN. DAR PINE
- BACKSAW
- MEDIUM AND FINE SANDPAPER
- COMBINATION SQUARE
- DRILL WITH COUNTERSINK AND 1/4-IN. BITS
- 16 x 2 3/8-IN., No. 6 COUNTERSINK SCREWS (NON-RUSTING)
- WOODSTAIN, CLEAR VARNISH, OR WAX
- BRUSH

PROJECT ONE

Pine duckboard

Say goodbye to soggy bathmats or standing in a puddle on a wet floor by making yourself this little deck to stand on when you get out of the shower. This duckboard is made from pine softwood, which is very easy to cut. The lengths can be sanded smooth and colored with an exterior-quality woodstain, or just varnished to seal the surface.

This practical and stylish duckboard is easy to make from pine softwood, and finished with wood stain or simply varnished.

HOW TO DO IT

STEP 1 Cut all the lengths of lumber, then sand any sharp edges to round them off slightly. Pay particular attention to the sawed ends.

STEP 2 Line the lengths up and mark the positions for the two cross-pieces.

STEP 3 Drill a countersunk clearance hole for a screw at each end of all the lengths, and screw the lengths to the cross-pieces.

STEP 4 Stain, wax, or simply varnish the duckboard. Apply the wax with a soft, lint-free cloth, leave to dry for 20 minutes, then buff with steel wool.

PROJECT TWO

A customized shower curtain

YOU WILL NEED:
• PLAIN COLORED PLASTIC OR NYLON SHOWER CURTAIN FITTED WITH A SET OF RINGS
• LIGHTWEIGHT FABRIC THE SAME SIZE AS THE CURTAIN OR, IF WIDER, IT CAN BE HEMMED
• APPLIQUÉ DAISIES
• FABRIC GLUE OR NEEDLE AND THREAD

Plastic shower curtains aren't the most attractive sight in a shower room, but only one side of the shower curtain needs to be water-repellent, so why not use cheap plastic curtain trimmings as the lining for something more in keeping with your own bathroom style? The curtain is only fixed to the liner at the top, above

the level where it will come into contact with any water, so the stitch perforations will not be a problem. Any lightweight fabric that is not too prone to creasing is suitable for this project, and the decorative additions are up to you. The daisies can be stuck to the fabric with a good fabric glue, or hand-stitched if you prefer.

Practical plastic shower curtains can be made into attractive versions with just a covering of fabric, a choice of decorations, and a sewing machine.

HOW TO DO IT

STEP 1 If the fabric is too wide, then cut it and hem it to match the size of the shower curtain. Measure the length against the shower curtain and sew a small hem at the top and bottom.

STEP 2 Line up the top of the cotton curtain with the top of the plastic curtain. Stitch the two together just below the holes for the shower rings. Use matching thread so that the stitches are invisible.

STEP 3 Arrange the daisies all over the curtain in a random "natural" lawn pattern. Stick them onto the fabric with the fabric glue and leave until it has dried and bonded. If you prefer, they can be slipstitched in place.

YOU WILL NEED:

• A NICE PLANK OF
  WOOD, ABOUT
  20 x 4 IN.
  DRIFTWOOD IS IDEAL,
  BUT NEW WOOD
  WITH AN INTERESTING
  GRAIN, SUCH AS AN
  OFF-CUT OF PARANÁ
  PINE OR A FRUIT
  WOOD, WOULD ALSO
  LOOK GOOD. ASK A
  LUMBER MERCHANT
  WHAT SUITABLE OFF-
  CUTS THEY HAVE,
  EXPLAINING THE USE
  IT WILL BE PUT TO.
  YOU MAY ALSO LIKE
  TO STAIN AND
  VARNISH THE WOOD.
• SOAP DISH
• 2 HOOKS
• DRILL
• 3/4-IN. TILE BIT
• PAINTER'S TAPE
• MARKER PEN
• SPIRIT LEVEL
• NON-RUSTING
  SCREWS TO ATTACH
  THE HOOKS (MOST
  COME WITH SCREWS)
• 2 x 3-IN. No. 10
  SCREWS TO FIX THE
  WOOD TO THE TILED
  WALL (THE SCREW
  LENGTH DEPENDS
  UPON THE DEPTH
  OF YOUR WOOD)
• WALL ANCHORS
• BRASS CUPPED
  SCREWS
• BRADAWL

PROJECT THREE

Shower caddy

Trying to locate the soap, shampoo, or sponge can be highly frustrating when water is cascading into your eyes. This simple solution should help to keep everything you need in one place, close to hand when you need it. It is ideally suited to a tiled wall, and its beauty lies in the fact that only two holes are drilled through the tiling, with the rest going into the wooden support.

This shower caddy lets you have a range of fittings with only two holes drilled through the tiles. All the rest are drilled to the wooden caddy.

HOW TO DO IT

STEP 1 Find the ideal position for the caddy on the shower wall, making quite sure that there are no pipes behind the tiles where the screws will be located! Mark the positions for the components and the shelf.

STEP 2 Drill two evenly spaced holes in the shelf end.

STEP 3 Screw the top shelf to the back plank using brass cupped screws. Screw the hooks and soap dish into position.

STEP 4 Place the unit in position on the wall. Mark through the pre-drilled holes onto the wall using a bradawl.

STEP 5 Drill holes through the tiles using a tile bit. Insert wall anchors.

STEP 6 Screw the unit to the wall using the brass cupped screws.

Fun & study

Working from home is many people's dream—no traffic jams, no train delays, no office politics. But whether you're going to be working from home full-time or just a few hours a week, your work area needs to be carefully planned so that you can switch from a domestic to a work environment without one intruding on the other. Home offices are also an opportunity to have fun with design—at last you don't have to put up with grey metal filing cabinets because your office is to suit you, and you alone. This section shows how to create stylish working spaces, either in separate offices or in part of a living area. It also looks at creating a teenager's study and a child's playroom.

Office-living space

The keyword in home office design is flexibility, and nowhere more so than in a room that serves several purposes. Ideally you want to be able to put away the working day without a trace of it left in the evening, and to start again effortlessly the next morning. This might seem like a tall order, but with so many of us choosing to work from home there is a wealth of design expertise in this area. It is now possible to buy fantastic pieces of furniture that look like stylish wardrobes, sideboards, or bookshelves at night, but which open out into a full working office during the day. They have been designed so that a full desk with computers, bookshelves, and files can be closed without putting anything away. Wonders like this don't come cheap, but when you consider the cost of renting and fitting out an office, it puts the price into perspective.

Despite the age of the computer, a fair amount of paperwork means old-fashioned filing systems are not quite dead. If your home office is also your living room, it's worth making your filing system as attractive as possible.

If your office is to be at one end of the living room, a divider of some sort will allow the room to be used for both purposes at the same time. Modular cubed units are excellent for this, especially if you have a mixture of some open cubes and others with doors. Mix the cubes so that some face the office and some the living room. If you prefer something less solid, then a screen is the best idea. There are lots of different styles in the stores and catalogs including minimalist Japanese, decoratively carved Indian style, wrought iron, and bamboo and seagrass. Screens are not difficult to make, and the basic construction technique described in the Traditional Living Room section could be used to make a larger office screen. Another option is to fit a Venetian blind. It will add a sharp, efficient look to the office, and you can vary the level of exclusion from the rest of the room by adjusting the slats. At the end of the working day you have the option of lowering and closing it to block the view of the office.

It is a good idea to have your office equipment, including the desk, on casters. This allows you maximum flexibility because everything can be easily moved around or out of the room altogether if the occasion demands. A wall-mounted cupboard with sliding doors will look good and conceal loads of files, catalogs, and magazines, and a low sideboard is a perfect piece of dual-purpose furniture. If you have a dining room, you could use a dining table as your daytime desk and a sideboard for storing all your paperwork without anyone being any the wiser. It is only viable for tidy, organized people with very good memories.

The essentials

Top of the list is some sort of work surface, that may be a proper desk, or a table with a drawer unit. Begin by making a realistic list of all the things you will need in your home office, and if you use a computer, allow plenty of space for all the extra bits and pieces like Zip drives, scanners, and printers. Several stylish mail order companies have ranges of contemporary desk units with all the proper shelves, including a low keyboard shelf, which is advisable if you going to be using the computer everyday. Ideally the monitor should be at eye level and your arms should be level with the keyboard. Desks don't have to cost much at all, in fact they are often given away free when you buy a new computer. A pair of saw horses topped with a piece of MDF will also make a great desk, especially if you invest in one or two filing cabinets and drawer units on casters, which can be wheeled out of sight when the office is shut. A proper office chair is essential for anyone spending more than an hour a day sitting at a desk. Aim to spend as much money as you can on the chair, and economize elsewhere. To avoid backache and repetitive stress injury (RSI), which causes pain in your fingers and wrists, you should sit with a straight back, your feet flat on the floor and elbows at your side as you tap the keyboard.

Organization

If your working area also serves another purpose, it is more important than ever to be really well organized. Computers were supposed to take the place of paperwork, but that hasn't completely happened yet, and most of us find that we still need an old-fashioned filing system. Then there are pens, pencils, rules, paper clips, stationery, and all the bits and bobs relevant to your work. A strong set of shelves for reference books, box files, and magazines could be fitted with a blind to hide them when you're not working. And a smart set of matching boxes to keep on display is particularly useful for clearing away all your clutter at the end of each working day. A notice board and calendar are also essential if you are to keep track of appointments, and there are some excellent programs for the computer that act as Post-It notes and daily, weekly, and monthly diary pages.

THE PROJECTS
The project on the following pages is the ultimate in flexibility, allowing you to keep the clutter of a desk in organized compartments that can be put away after use.

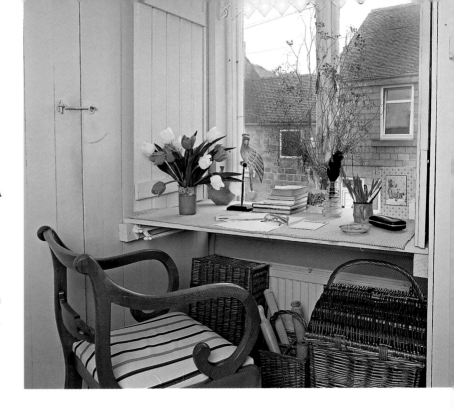

Lighting

The best light to work by is a directional light, angled to illuminate your desk area. In addition the room needs either good natural light, or artificial ambient light, for the evening or dull days, so that the contrast between the brightness of a computer screen and the rest of the room is never too great. Use overhead or wall lights to balance the lighting.

Pleasing yourself

One of the joys of working from home is that your office need not bear any resemblance to an office at all. So, be creative and remember that this is home first and an office second. A large wicker hamper is as good as a metal cupboard for keeping box files in, and polka-dotted tumblers can hold pencils and paper clips. Biscuit barrels hold several rolls of tape and balls of string, and a CD storage rack takes care of the CD-Roms and Zip disks. A typist's chair can be re-covered to match the curtains, a vase of flowers will do more for the desk top than any executive toy, and when the day's work is done, why not treat your computer like a birdcage and cover it with a large silk scarf?

A home office doesn't have to look like an office at all. Wicker hampers with compartments serve as useful storage space, and you can never go wrong with a vase of fresh flowers.

YOU WILL NEED:

- A SHEET OF $^3/_4$-IN. MDF CUT AS FOLLOWS:
  BACK 24 x 35 IN.
  TOP SHELF 12 x 35 IN.
  BOTTOM SHELF 9$^3/_4$ x 12 IN.
  SMALL SIDE SHELVES 6 x 6 IN. (2 PIECES)
  LEFT-HAND SIDE 24$^3/_8$ x 26 IN.
  RIGHT-HAND SIDE 24$^3/_8$ x 8 IN.
  LEFT UPRIGHTS 17$^5/_8$ x 12 IN. (2 PIECES)
  RIGHT UPRIGHTS 17$^5/_8$ x 6 IN. (2 PIECES)
- 1$^1/_2$-IN. No. 6 SCREWS
- WOOD GLUE
- WORKBENCH
- JIGSAW
- TAPE MEASURE
- COMBINATION SQUARE
- CARPENTER'S PENCIL
- DRILL WITH PILOT, SCREW, AND COUNTERSINK BITS (USE SIZE 4 SCREWSINK BIT FOR ALL THREE)
- LONG RULE
- SANDPAPER

When this desktop unit is sat on a table, it creates an instant work surface. It keeps all your desktop clutter in an organized space, which can be quickly put away after use.

PROJECT ONE

A desktop unit

The work surface can be a table or simply a sheet of thick board supported on a pair of saw horses, but what turns it into an efficient desk are the drawer units, shelves, and storage space. This project shows how to build a free- standing unit to sit on top of the work surface. It includes space for the computer monitor, storage for CD-Roms and discs, two file compartments, a stationery tray compartment, and a book-ended shelf on the top.

HOW TO DO IT

STEP 1 Hold the uprights, dividers, and shelves against the back section, and mark out their positions in pencil on the back.

STEP 2 Draw, cut, and sand the mitered corners on the two sides.

STEP 3 Measure and draw a 6-in.-square box at the bottom of the central section on the back piece. This will be cut out to serve as a channel for the computer cables.

STEP 4 Use a jigsaw to cut out the cable box and the top shelf shape.

STEP 5 Drill clearance holes on the back section, and countersink.

STEP 6 Fix the uprights to the back section.

STEP 7 Fix the sides to the two uprights. Fix the smaller shelves to the sides and back.

STEP 8 Fill the holes, sand, and paint in your chosen color.

Use this sketch to help you construct your desk. Remember to measure all the lumber accurately, and use a spirit level to ensure that everything is level.

Home office
Computers have revolutionized our world to the point where many more of us now work from home. Why spend time commuting to and from the office when everything can be done here and not there? And if that's the route you are taking, it really is worth designing and decorating your new office.

The first thing you need to do when planning a new office in your home is to decide what you will use it for, how often, and what equipment you will need to keep in it. Then you can look at what you would like in your home office, as well as what you will need. As the boss, you're in the lucky position of making all the decisions, so don't feel constrained by any preconceived ideas of how an office should or shouldn't look. Six things to consider when planning your home office are...

When space is at a premium, or you only plan to work at home part-time, an area underneath the staircase can be an ideal working space.

Location
A spare bedroom or a dining room are the rooms most likely to be turned into an office, but when space is at a premium you could make use of a landing or even a cupboard under the stairs. A lot depends upon how many of you share the home—if you're on your own or a couple, it will be a lot easier to set the office boundaries than if you have a family. Working from home with young children is not impossible, but it is a challenge.

If you have an attic, garage, or outhouse with conversion potential, then it is worth finding out what it will cost. If you plan to work from home in the long term, then an office slightly removed from the home environment could be the perfect solution. If you are only planning to work a few hours a day, though, then you could make do with a very small but highly organized work area, and the space under the stairs is not as funny as it sounds. The idea is not to disappear into a cupboard and close the door behind you, but to think of your office as part of an open-plan design. The best scenario is where the stairs run up the side of the room. Your desk, storage, filing, and bookshelves can be tucked into the space underneath the staircase while you actually sit in the room facing it, without being claustrophobic!

If you are at work in complete isolation, then arrange everything to suit yourself, but if you expect to see visitors, then the office should be as close to the front door as possible to minimize domestic intrusion. Maintaining a professional attitude is difficult enough at home without having strangers peering at your unmade beds and unwashed breakfast plates.

Electricity

One of the first things to consider is, do you need more electric and phone sockets? The fax and internet connections are best on a separate line so that they don't interfere with the home phone number. In fact new phone line options are being introduced all the time, so seek advice from your phone company. With sockets, the basic strips can take four plugs, but you can also buy a more expensive version with eight sockets and two phone sockets. Be generous with your socket allowance so that you avoid trailing cables in the work area. Computers should also be plugged into surge protectors, which block destructive power surges during electrical storms. Plan your lighting at this stage too, so that your work area is well lit and the rest of the room has a pleasant ambient lighting system. Having a good background light level prevents eye strain from a bright computer screen. Daylight bulbs mimic natural light and are reputed to be easier on the eyes, and getting the lighting right keeps you alert and prevents tiredness.

Fitting and furnishing

A flick through an office supplier's catalog will show you that there isn't just a gadget for everything, but different versions of each gadget. So be assured that whatever your special office needs, they can be met. And if it's just a desk, chair, and filing cabinet that you're after, they also come in a huge range of styles and prices.

Spend as much money as you can afford on a good adjustable chair, one that assures you of having the right posture when you're working.

Ideally your back should be straight, with the lumbar region of your spine well supported, thighs parallel to the floor, and both feet flat on the ground. This may mean having a raised foot rest under your feet if you are not working at an ergonomically designed computer desk. To find out what the correct posture feels like, simply place a few books under your feet and a rolled towel in the small of your back.

Fully adjustable office chairs have levers for tilting and altering the seat and back support height. Since they can be very expensive, it really is worth looking in a secondhand office supplies store. And because businesses regularly close down or have a change in office style, second-hand does not necessarily mean worn-out. Filing cabinets, letter trays, and drawer units are other potentially expensive items that can be bought secondhand and given a makeover to match your home-office style. In fact these stores can be real

A good adjustable office chair is one item of furniture you cannot afford to be without. Secondhand chairs can be just as good as new, so it doesn't need to break the bank.

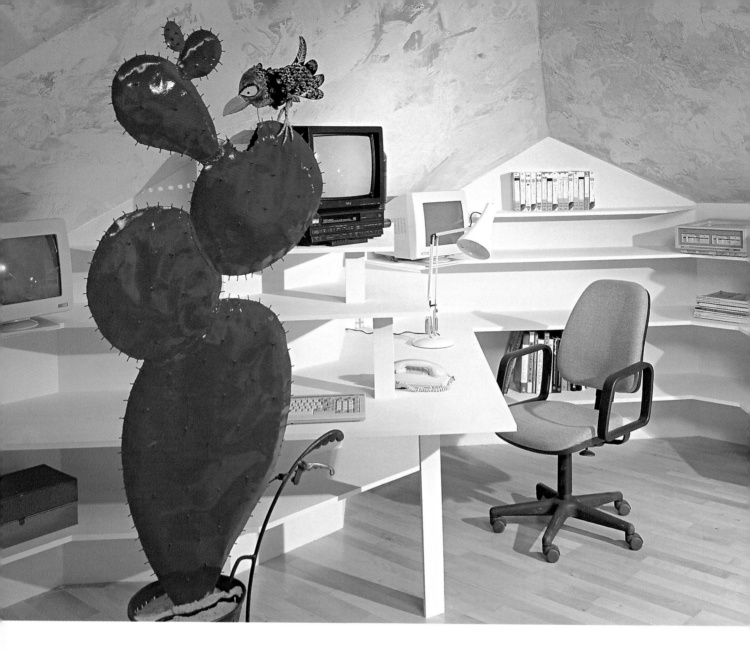

Aladdin's caves, and you never know what you'll find. There is no need to surround yourself with dull, utilitarian gray or beige metal cabinets just because they are the only colors on offer. Buy the poor dull things and inject a bit of fun by giving them an uplifting color change with metal primer and enamel paints from an auto accessory store. If meetings or interviews are part of your work, then you will also need to provide seating for your visitors. A lot depends on your line of work, and if it is quite buzzy and informal then stools would be fine, otherwise consider a smart compact sofa-bed, and then you will even be able to offer friends a bed for the night!

Walls

Decorating the home office should encourage you to spend time in there without any distractions. One of the most difficult aspects of working from home is being able to disengage yourself from any domestic jobs that need doing. The very last thing you need is to be constantly looking round and thinking that the room could do with a good coat of paint and a new set of curtains. Concentrate on work. You haven't time for all that! Get the decorating done after the electrics and before the arrival of heavy desks and cupboards. Keep the style simple and wall colors light to make the most of the daylight, and don't be afraid to use white, which looks good with everything. Light colors expand spaces and prevent the office from looking crowded once all the equipment is in place.

Windows

When choosing a window treatment for your office, it is quite important to choose something that won't look out of place with the rest of your home when seen from the outside. Slatted blinds are the most versatile option because they can be adjusted to admit maximum daylight, filter bright sunlight, and block views, giving good security. They also look cool and contemporary. Vertical blinds are being used a lot more in homes these days, and they do a similar job but with broader vertical slats.

Floors

When it comes to flooring, you have the choice of a carpet or hard surface. As ever, your choice must be guided by your kind of work. Vinyl or linoleum is the most hardwearing and easy to clean, and it also has the advantage over carpet when casters are being used. Cork is inexpensive and is coming back into fashion, particularly the dark, stained version. The other hard flooring option is a laminated floating floor. It comes in different quality grades and two basic designs.

PROJECTS
The three projects on the following pages focus on three essential parts of any home office: lighting, storage, and, of course, the desk space. But to make the most of the freedom allowed by the home office, the emphasis is on fun as well as function, allowing a bit of creativity to be added to the work environment. A fresh coat of paint, a little disciplined filing, and a big vase of flowers should do the rest.

Both follow the tongue-and-groove style, with one type needing glue to join the planks, and the other using an interlocking design. The second type can be lifted and moved. If you choose carpet, it is a good idea to buy a clear plastic chair mat that will allow you to move and swivel easily around your desk area.

Wardrobes can be made into stationery cupboards or complete workstations. At the end of the day, the doors can be closed on anything resembling work.

YOU WILL NEED:
- 4 x 1-IN. LUMBER FOR BOX FRAME
- ADHESIVE
- THIN ACRYLIC SHEET FOR FRONT
- ½-IN. MDF FOR BASE
- DRILL
- FLUORESCENT STRIPLIGHT TO FIT THE BOX SIZE
- ARROW SHAPE CUT OUT OF CARD
- CRAFT KNIFE
- ADHESIVE SPRAY
- 2 MIRROR FIXINGS
- RIGHT-ANGLED MOLDING
- SPRAY GLUE
- BACKSAW AND MITER BLOCK

PROJECT ONE

Lighting

If you are converting a bedroom or dining room into an office, the chances are that you will have to completely rethink the lighting. The two types of lighting needed are ambient, which is the background lighting all around you, and task lighting, which is directional lighting illuminating your work area. If you also have a seating area for clients, this could be lit from above with a pendant lamp. This project shows how to light an office area.

We are all familiar with light boxes, usually with the message "EXIT" on them. This project is a bit of fun along these lines. Use two dark-colored pieces of cardboard cut in arrow shapes, which will show through the acrylic sheet. The glass is then assembled in a box frame with a fluorescent tube.

An exit sign with a difference! This novel light box uses an acrylic sheet in front of a fluorescent light tube. You can design your own pattern or lettering for a personal touch.

HOW TO DO IT

STEP 1 Have the white acrylic sheet cut to size, and then cut the wood to size and sand the edges. Make a simple butt-jointed box, glue, and screw the joints.

STEP 2 Cut out the right-angle molding, using a backsaw and miter block.

STEP 3 Place the acrylic sheet on top of the box. Drill clearance holes through the molding and screw it to the sheet and the box frame.

STEP 4 Cut out the arrow shapes. Spray glue onto the back and stick to the acrylic sheet in the inside of the box.

STEP 5 Drill an exit hole for the cable in the back or the side of the box, and place the fitting and bulb inside the box.

STEP 6 Screw the back of the box in place, add the bulb and fixings and attach to the wall. Paint if desired.

TIP
* You can use any motif or word in your light box—just choose something that is personal to you.

YOU WILL NEED:
- 1 SHEET OF
  3/4-IN. MDF
- LONG RULE
- TAPE MEASURE
- COMBINATION
  SQUARE
- PENCIL
- DRILL
- PILOT BIT AND
  COUNTERSINK BIT
- SCREWS

PROJECT TWO

Storage

There is no getting away from storage. Whatever type of work you do, paperwork mounts up, records must be kept, and we all need somewhere to keep telephone books and reference material. This storage unit on casters will take care of books, files, and catalogs. The top is at desk height, so with a piece of MDF laid on top it provides an extra work surface.

This handy storage unit on casters keeps books, files, and catalogs accessible at the same time as neatly stored away. An optional top surface of MDF will make an additional work surface.

HOW TO DO IT

STEP 1 Cut the back of the unit from the sheet of MDF. It should be the height of your desk minus the height of the casters if you want to extend the desk area. Cut out all the shelves, dividers, and the top, sides, and bottom of the unit.

STEP 2 Draw the positions of the sides, top, and bottom, and all the partitions and shelves in pencil on the back. Use a length of MDF to do this so that you can see a flat plan of the unit on the back.

STEP 3 Drill clearance holes to fix all the pieces to the back of the unit. Hold each piece in position as you drill through the clearance holes to make pilot holes for the screws.

STEP 4 Assemble the outer frame first, applying wood glue to the joining edges before screwing them together through the back. Drill pilot, clearance, and countersink holes, then secure the corner joints by screwing them together. Fit all the partitions in place first, and then add the shelves. Drill, glue, and screw each one so that the whole unit stands firm.

STEP 5 Finally drill holes and fit the four casters onto the base of the unit.

STEP 6 Sand all the sharp edges smooth, then paint if required, or use it just as it is.

YOU WILL NEED:
• SHEET OF 1-IN. MDF
• 4 DESK LEGS
• DRILL AND $^3/_{32}$-IN. BIT
• JIGSAW
• PATTERN
• PENCIL
• 4 SQUARES OF WOOD
  TO MOUNT THE LEG
  FITTINGS ON

PROJECT THREE

Curved desk

You can make a very smart desk from one sheet of MDF and a pair of saw horses. Or you can buy the legs in sets of four, as shown in this project, which are then simply attached to the underside of the desk. This desk is ideal for someone whose desk is always piled high, because it is shaped like a curve, so when you sit at it, everything is within arm's reach.

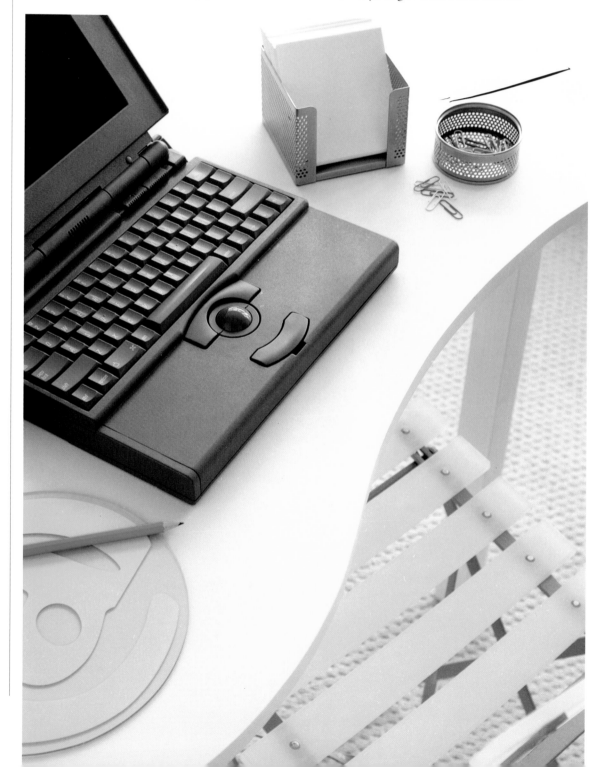

A simple curved desk made out of MDF is both stylish and functional. You can either buy a pair of saw horses or four, ready-made legs.

HOW TO DO IT

STEP 1 Support the MDF between two saw horses. Draw the curve in pencil, either from a pattern or to your own plan. Cut out the curve with a jigsaw, and sand.

STEP 2 Support the desk leg in the work bench and drill a vertical hole for fitting.

STEP 3 The leg fittings consist of two parts—one post with a screw fitting to fit into the leg, and one to receive the post, which fits under the table top.

STEP 4 Screw the squares of wood to the underneath of the table, then mark the positions for the legs and all their screws. Drill pilot holes using a 3/32-in. drill bit.

STEP 5 Screw the top receiving plate of the leg fitting into the wood boss.

STEP 6 Screw each leg into position. Lift the table and turn. Seal the surfaces with MDF primer or a 50:50 dilution of PVA and water. Paint, or stain and varnish the desk.

TIP
* These table legs are sold in packs
in hardware stores, and always have instructions
included with them. If you prefer, you could
use saw horse legs, which can
also be found in hardware stores.

202

Teenager's study
Creating an environment to encourage a teenage to study is an interesting challenge, and one solution is to put the emphasis on relaxation, keeping a corner that is conducive to study. The best way to do this is to build in a worktop with all the shelving, drawers, and electrical sockets that the teenager will need for computers, CDs, and video games. There is little point in excluding these things, because the object is to get children to spend time in the room and make studying easier. Exclusion simply makes forbidden fruit taste sweeter.

The great thing about the DIY boom is that there is a close link between fashion and decorating styles, with top clothes designers also designing home furnishing ranges. This means that teenagers today are far more conscious of interior design fashions than most of us were at their age. The key to success lies in parent and child working together as a team, doing everything from planning and shopping to actually making the changes. Sometimes, as parents we think it is easier to get on and do the work ourselves, but if we do that we are denying our kids the satisfaction of

The best studies for teenagers are those that also include an element of relaxation and entertainment, to entice them into the work area.

working hard and joining in. Begin by asking for a wish list of everything they would have if money were no object, then set a budget and help to edit what is on the list. Try to include an extravagance or two like a fake fur beanbag or a really cool anglepoise lamp. Discuss color, furniture, lighting, and flooring, and look at as many style magazines as you can find. Keep a look out for special features flagged on the front of home magazines, and buy any for home offices, studies, or bedsits. If your teenager is likely to go to college, then this room could build a bridge between their childhood and future independence.

Practicalities
If you are giving this room a makeover together, it is important that the whole process doesn't drag on too long, so stick to a time limit. Paint the walls one weekend, and hire an electrician to fit extra plugs and sort out the lighting at the same time. When it comes to the flooring, the best tip is to use expensive underlay and cheap carpeting. The underlay will cut the noise level dramatically, and the carpet can be replaced once your fledgling has flown the nest. A tough cord carpet can always be softened by a large rug for lounging on.

Once the carpet is down, the workstation can be built. It should be custom-made to meet your teenager's specific needs. Drawer units on casters are a good idea because they allow for more flexibility. And make the desktop wide and long enough, with ample shelving for magazines and reference books, with smaller shelves for CDs and games. Fit strip lighting under the shelving, and an anglepoise light on the worktop. If the area looks business-like, they will be more likely to get down to work. Set aside an amount in the budget for folders, boxes, files, notebooks, and a new mouse mat for the computer.

You should also buy a comfortable, adjustable office chair to encourage good posture. Most furniture stores stock them, and it is also worth having a look at secondhand office furniture stores because they deal with businesses that close down, so secondhand does not have to mean old and ratty.

Comfort zone
Once the work side of the room has been taken care of, you can turn your attention to the comfort zone. Seating can be soft and low with cushions and beanbags. If you have an old sofa to put in the room, it can be covered with a fleece throw. Fleece comes in a wide range of colors and has the bonus of requiring no hemming—and washes really well. Fake fur fabrics also make great throws, and are not expensive to buy by the yard. A decorator's cotton dustsheet covers most sofas, and can be machine-dyed to the color of your teenager's choice.

Coffee table
A low coffee table can be made from recycled wooden pallets. This wood is rough but soft, and is easy to smooth with an electric sander. The table surface can be faced with a sheet of hardboard edged with domed upholstery tacks, and four large casters will give it a contemporary edge. Another option is to head down to the secondhand stores and find something to make over.

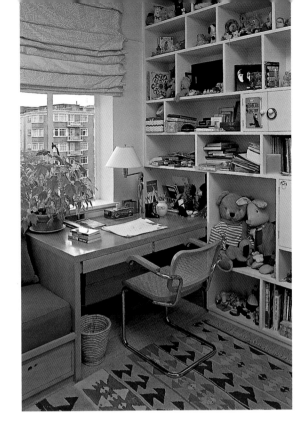

Teenagers need storage space too, especially if their study is part of their bedroom. Make sure they have enough places to put everything, so they have no excuse for not tidying up.

Window dressing
Blinds or shutters that block out the daylight are usually popular with this age group. A room should be as dark as a nightclub first thing in the morning. Roller blinds with black-out backing work best if they are fitted into the window frame recess.

Fridge
And to finish off, include a small refrigerator. It may seem like a luxury, but it makes sense if long hours are to be spent working and relaxing in the room. Look for a studio or trailer fridge that will not take up too much space in the room, and give it a color lift with auto spray paints. It will be the height of cool!

PROJECTS
The four projects on the following pages combine a sense of work with relaxation, to make a teenager's study as appealing as possible. Make sure you work as a team from the start, so that personal touches can be added along the way.

Worktop

The big advantage of making a desk is that it can be made to fit the person and their specific requirements. If the desk is to be used for, say, a sewing machine as well as a computer, the sockets should be sited in a convenient position for both uses with all electrical cables channeled behind the unit. When you plan a unit to your own specifications, it can be easily fitted under a sloping ceiling or in an alcove. This plan is for building a worktop into a corner; the right type of shelves can be attached to the wall above it.

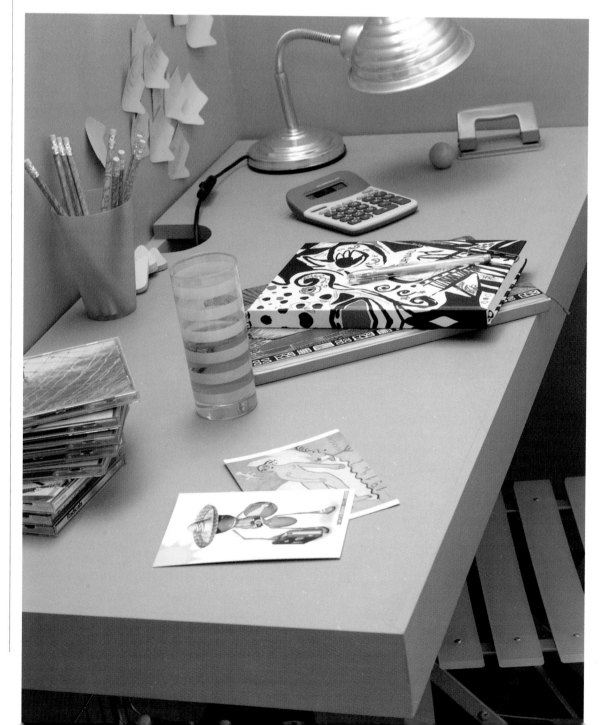

A worktop made specially for teenagers can be painted in their favorite colors, making work seem less of a chore.

HOW TO DO IT

STEP 1 Decide upon the length and depth of the worktop, and then cut the lumber to fit. Mark the position and height of the table on the wall. Use a spirit level to check the level.

STEP 2 Drill clearance holes through the battens approximately 10 in. apart, and then hold them up to the wall and mark their positions in pencil. Drill and plug the holes in the wall, and then screw the battens in place.

STEP 3 Cut the leg to the correct height. You will need an extra pair of hands to support it while you rest the batten on top; check that it is level before screwing it to the wall batten. Now add the final batten that completes the frame for the worktop. Check that it is level before screwing it to the leg and the wall batten.

STEP 4 Cut the sheet of MDF to fit the top exactly, and then cut out a channel at the back of the worktop to take all the electrical cables down to the socket. Sand smooth.

STEP 5 Drill clearance holes, then screw the top to the battens and the legs.

STEP 6 Measure two fascia strips to fit on to the front and side of the worktop. Mitering the ends where they meet will give a more professional finish. Apply wood glue, and then secure the strips with brads, using the small hammer. Sand, prime, and paint the legs and fascia strips. The worktop can be protected with two coats of varnish, or a coat of paint. If you varnish the top, then run a line of painter's tape along its edge when you paint the fascia to guarantee a really straight line.

YOU WILL NEED:
- PEGBOARD OR SOFTBOARD
- MOLDING FOR FRAME SURROUND
- MITER SAW TO CUT FRAME CORNERS
- DRILL, WALL ANCHORS AND SCREWS TO FIX THE FRAME TO THE WALL
- PANEL ADHESIVE FOR SOFTBOARD
- 1-IN. X 1-IN. BATTENS FOR PEGBOARD
- HARDBOARD PINS AND SMALL HAMMER FOR THE PEGBOARD

PROJECT TWO

Pegboard or softboard wall covering

Pegboard is perforated hardboard that can be used to cover sections or complete walls. It not only looks good, retro, and funky, but provides a really useful storage surface. The holes are used for hooks and pegs for hanging containers, small boxes, speakers, and other gizmos. An alternative, useful, and inexpensive material is softboard, which is usually used as a liner for school corridor walls. It is very lightweight, and can be stuck onto the wall with panel adhesive and then painted for use as a notice board.

Softboard makes an ideal noticeboard because it is lightweight, so it can be stuck on the wall with panel adhesive and painted a favorite color. A few pin-ups and other teenage collectables will do the rest.

HOW TO DO IT

STEP 1 Hold the softboard against the wall and mark the position of the corners. Apply panel adhesive to the back of the softboard, and stick it onto the wall.

STEP 2 Hold the molding up to the wall and mark the position of the miters. Drill clearance holes in three places along the length of each side. Mark the screw positions on the walls, and then drill and plug. Apply panel adhesive to the back of the moldings and screw them to the wall.

STEP 3 Paint the softboard to blend in or contrast with the wall color. Two coats may be necessary, because it is highly absorbent.

YOU WILL NEED:
- HUBCAP
- DRILL
- CLOCK MOVEMENT AND HANDS
- BATTERY
- STEEL WOOL
- DETERGENT
- STICKY DOTS

PROJECT THREE

A hubcap clock

Making clocks is incredibly easy, costs very little, and you can use any image you like for the face, including a photograph of someone or a hubcap! For a graphic effect, apply brightly colored sticky dots to the clock face instead of numerals. You will also need a battery-powered movement and a pair of hands, which come in a range of styles.

It is easier than you might think to make a clock, and you can make one out of almost anything. All you need is a clock movement with hands and your choice of "clock face" (in this case, a hubcap), and you're there!

HOW TO DO IT

STEP 1 Clean off any dirt using steel wool and detergent.

STEP 2 Drill a hole in the center of the hubcap for the clock movement.

STEP 3 Add the sticky dots to mark the hours.

STEP 4 Place the mechanism in the back and add the clock hands.

YOU WILL NEED:
- 30-IN. EACH OF ORANGE AND BLACK (OR ANY COLORS) OF FLEECE FABRIC
- THREAD
- SEWING MACHINE
- NEEDLE FOR HAND STITCHING
- BAG OF FOAM CHIPPINGS OR TWO PILLOWS PER CUSHION

PROJECT FOUR

Floor cushions

If you have a sewing machine and can sew in a straight line, there is no reason to buy large, expensive cushions. The best fabric for this sort of thing is fleece. It is inexpensive, comes in a wide range of funky colors, and is something of a miracle because it is made from recycled plastic bottles! Buy 30-in. lengths of two different colors and then cut the two lengths in half. This will make two 30-in.-square cushions, and you can use both colors on each cushion.

Fleece cushion covers are perfect for lounging on a study floor after a hard few hours' studying. Fleece is a cheap fabric that comes in a huge range of funky colors.

HOW TO DO IT

STEP 1 Place one dark and one light square together with fluffy sides facing. Sew a line of stitches about 1 in. inside the outer edge, but leave a 4-in. gap for stuffing. Do the same with both cushions.

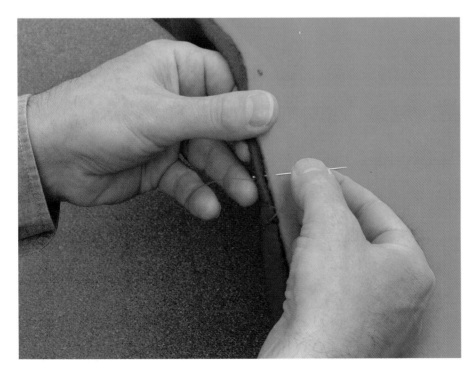

STEP 2 Fill the cushions with foam chips or a pair of pillows, and then use small slip stitches to close the gaps. Could anything be simpler?

Child's playroom

If you have space for a playroom in your home, then everyone is a winner. The children will love having their own activity room, and you will be able to gear their bedrooms toward relaxation and sleep, avoiding reminders of daytime excitement. A playroom is not just for kids, though, it is somewhere for parents to relax with their children and friends without worrying about dangers or mess. The trick is to design a playroom that is virtually indestructible and danger-free, without making it look like a padded cell!

A children's playroom is a perfect excuse for letting your imagination run wild. This playroom has been transformed into an exciting Wild West setting, complete with its very own jailhouse.

To do this you design with children in mind, excluding things like slippery floors, sharp corners, tall but not out of reach shelving, trailing electric cables, and doors that can slam on small fingers. It is not that you want a child who is unaware of danger and is incapable of recognizing it, but more that the playroom should be a sanctuary from it. Somewhere to let off steam. A place to be happy and uninhibited. Top 10 things to have in a great playroom might be…

Vinyl flooring

A cushioned vinyl floor with a good quality underlay and a non-slip surface is the best flooring for a playroom. It has all the necessary qualities. Kids can safely scoot around, rollerskate, play with cars, fall on their knees, and spill their drinks, while you have an easy-clean surface.

Bean bags

The original beanbag has been downsized for kids, and the same idea has been taken a stage further to make little armchairs with beanbag filling. Kids love sitting or lolling about in beanbags, and there are no hard edges to bump themselves on. As a security measure, stitch the metal end of the zip flat onto the fabric cover to prevent the ultimate snowstorm when the little darlings discover how to fling out the polystyrene beads!

Sofa

The comfortable sofa is for the adults. This is where you sit with your friends, or with a child on your knee, watching a video or telling a story. An inexpensive sofa with a removable, washable cover in a bright color is the ideal choice.

TV and video

A television in a playroom may seem something of a contradiction, but television is definitely part of a young child's experience. If the television is surrounded by more hands-on, tempting things to do, then it will not always win the battle for the child's attention. Sometimes children are soothed by the repetition of their favorite story or cartoon video, or want to watch them with their friends. The television can always be kept behind doors if you prefer not have it on show all the time.

Worktop for painting and drawing

Children love to paint and draw, and they need access to paper, paints, and crayons. They learn the rudiments at kindergarten, and will delight in endlessly painting their favorite subjects. You will need one or two low tables and chairs, an easel, paint pots, large brushes, anti-spill beakers for water and paints, wax crayons, aprons, and a washing line with pegs to hang up the pictures to dry. Colored paper, glue, and safe scissors are the other must-haves.

Construction area

Children play with all kinds of building sets, beginning with basic wooden blocks before moving on to wooden trains, snap-together plastic bricks, and miniature models of everything from galleons to spacecraft. The most important thing to know about construction toys is that each type must be kept separate, otherwise they are never played with. This inevitably means a lot of hard sorting for parents, but make life easier by having an efficient storage system. Transparent plastic crates on casters are the perfect solution.

Blinds or curtains

The playroom will mostly be used in the daytime, but it is still nice to have the option of cutting out the daylight by pulling down the blinds or drawing the curtains. They are particularly useful for afternoon naps on the settee, a game of hide-

Each set of games and construction toys needs to be kept separate, or they will never be played with.

and-seek, shutting out the rain, or reducing
dazzling sunshine. And winter evenings always
seem more cozy with the curtains drawn.

Sink

If there is a water source nearby, have the pipes
diverted and install a sink in the playroom. You
will not regret it. It means that children can be
cleaned up after painting, eating, or accidents
without leaving the room. The paint pots and
brushes can be washed, cloths can be wrung
out under the tap, and all this without leaving
the playroom. A low square sink is ideal, but
do have a thermostat on the hot tap to prevent
scalds. Another good idea is to keep the plug
on a high shelf to avert any catastrophic floods!

Easy-reach storage

One way to make short work of tidying up is
to build a boxed seat along one wall, with doors
hinged along their top edge, instead of on the
side. They can then be lifted up like garage doors
for putting boxes away. Another storage idea is to
have a rail with pegs for hanging bags—plastic
mesh bags are good because the contents are
visible. Buy the storage crates first, and build the
shelves to fit them. It is also essential to have out-

of-reach storage for art materials, a first-aid kit,
face paints, board games, and jigsaw puzzles—
everything that you have out.

Bright lights

There is a difference between bright and harsh,
and what you want is bright, jolly lighting that
makes it easy to find things, read books, paint
pictures, and play games. One or two 100-watt
overhead pendant lights will illuminate the room,
and a dimmer switch can be used to lower the
light for quiet times. Anglepoise lights are useful
for illuminating worktops, but use screw fittings
to secure the lamp onto a shelf, and avoid any
type of lamp that could be knocked over.

When decorating the playroom, include one
area of wall painted with blackboard paint. This is
guaranteed to be one of the most popular places
in the room. Supply a large box of colored chalks
and a damp cloth to clean the board. Paint the
other walls with bright, cheerful colors and use as
many special effects as you can find. Glitter glazes
and scented paints are just two fun finishes that
kids will love. And one of the following projects
shows how to print a mural using foam blocks. It
couldn't be easier or more effective. Deciding
whether to allow children to help with the
decorating is up to you—there are definite pros
and cons (it can be difficult for a young child to
understand why it's OK to paint on the walls in
one room, but not in another!). The floor project
shows how to stencil a bold pattern of stripes,
balls, and stars on a painted wooden floor. This
could also be done with vinyl floor paints to cheer
up an existing vinyl floor. In a big room, the floor
can be treated like a playground and painted with
a roadway, hopscotch, snakes and ladders, or
another favorite game. Let your imagination run
wild, and remember that the more fun you have
while decorating, the better it will look.

PROJECT ONE

Mural printed with large foam blocks

Children have been building toy towns from shaped wooden blocks for a very long time, and this project does the same thing in two dimensions instead of three. Look out for a store selling upholstery foam, and buy off-cuts. They are easy to cut with a snap-blade knife if you make the first cut along a drawn line, then bend the foam to open the cut, and cut through the rest of it. Limit yourself to five bold shapes—a large square, a small square, an oblong, a triangle, and an arch.

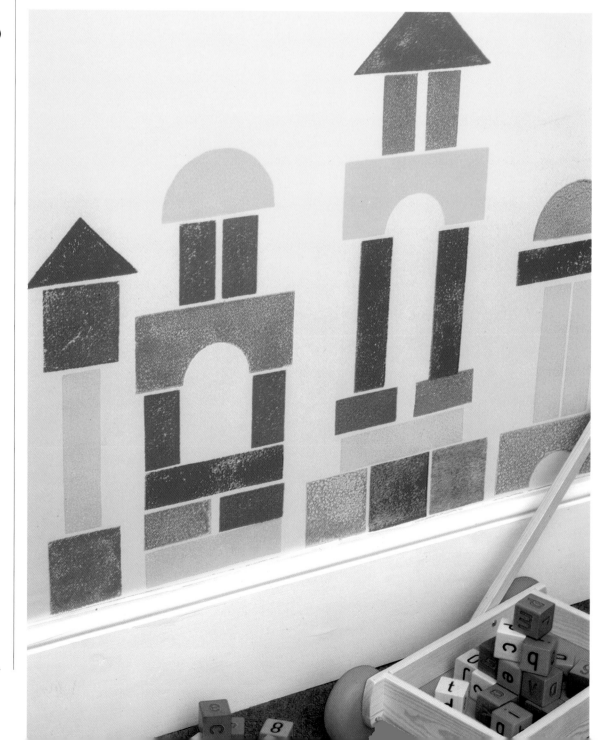

A colorful mural printed with foam blocks is far easier than a hand-drawn creation, but just as fun and inspirational.

HOW TO DO IT

STEP 1 Draw the pattern shapes onto card, using the set square and rule to draw the geometric shapes accurately. Draw generously sized shapes in proportion to the wall width and height. Stick the shapes to the foam.

STEP 2 Cut out the shapes. Make sure you have a sharp blade, and make the first cut in one go along the drawn line. The lower cuts to separate the foam pieces are not so important because they are not part of the printing surface.

STEP 3 Place a circle of each color on a plate, and mix in the same amount of pre-mixed wallpaper paste. This will make the paint more gelatinous, and stop it from running if you have too much paint on the foam.

STEP 4 Dampen the foam, squeeze out any excess moisture, and then begin to print. Press the block into the paint and test the print on a sheet of paper. Press the foam onto the wall to make a print. Build up the base blocks first.

STEP 5 Use the squares and oblongs to make a pair of pillars, and then print the arch shape over the top.

STEP 6 Top some of the squares with triangles, and keep on swapping the foam blocks and printing until the wall is covered with a toy town. A coat of clear varnish will help to protect and preserve the mural.

YOU WILL NEED:
- SHEET OF WAXED STENCIL CARD CUT INTO TWO 12-IN. SQUARES
- SNAP-BLADE KNIFE
- PHOTOCOPY OF EACH PATTERN
- ADHESIVE SPRAY
- LARGE STENCIL BRUSH
- TWO WHITE PLATES
- ABSORBENT PAPER TOWEL
- PAINT IN TWO CONTRASTING COLORS (EITHER LATEX AND VARNISH, OR A PREPARATORY FLOOR PAINT)
- CLEAR, STRONG POLYURETHANE VARNISH
- BRUSH TO APPLY THE VARNISH
- MINERAL SPIRITS TO CLEAN THE BRUSH

PROJECT TWO

Stenciling a floor border

Stenciling on the floor is really easy, and you never get the problem of paint running, as sometimes happens on walls. For this project you need a 12-in. square as the repeat, with two different shapes cut out of stencil card and alternated to form a border pattern around the edge of the room. This could be done on vinyl floor tiles with special vinyl paint, or using a latex paint with a varnish to seal it on wood. If you want a solid border, then paint a 12-in.-wide background color, or alternate two colors that can then be reversed for the pattern.

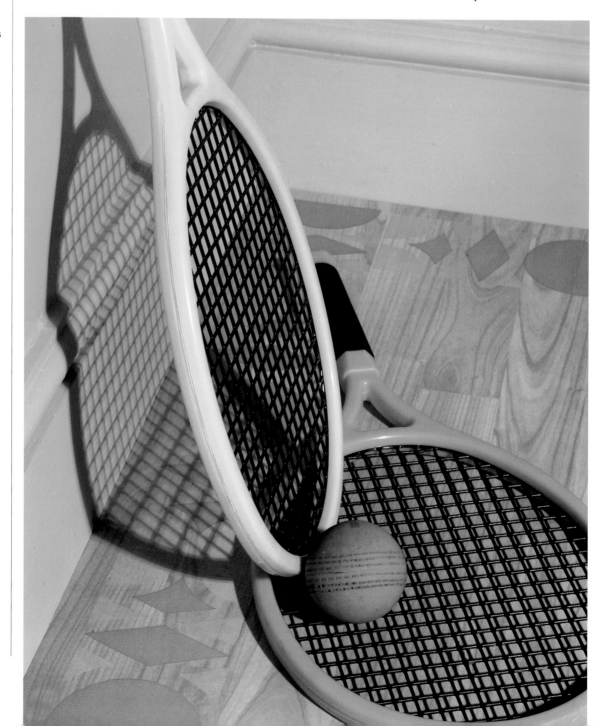

A stencil pattern border can brighten up either a wooden or a vinyl floor. For vinyl, use a special vinyl paint. Use a few repetitive patterns for a balanced, geometric effect.

HOW TO DO IT

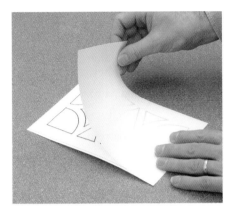

STEP 1 Photocopy the pattern so that it fills most of the stencil card—leave a ¾–1⅜-in. border around the edges so that the stencil is not too flimsy. Spray the back of the pattern with adhesive spray and stick it to the card.

STEP 2 Use a snap-blade knife to cut out the stencils carefully. Always cut outward from the corners, and try to cut curves with one even movement, to avoid jagged edges.

STEP 3 Spray the back of the stencil with adhesive spray and leave for 5 minutes. Put a blob of each color on the plates. You need a very small amount of paint for stenciling. Coat the brush with paint, and then dab most of it off on the paper towel.

STEP 4 Mark the guidelines in chalk if you are painting onto wooden floorboards, otherwise paint on to the colored background. Place the stencil on the floor and smooth it flat. Apply the first color.

STEP 5 Apply the second color in exactly the same way.

STEP 6 If you are painting a wooden floor with latex, apply 1–3 coats of varnish when the paint is bone-dry. Floor paint is tough enough not to need varnish.

Use this guide to help you cut out the pattern for the stencil, and position it on the correct place on your floor.

YOU WILL NEED:
- SHEET OF ¹⁄₂-IN. MDF
- 2 LEGS FOR THE FRONT
  OF THE WORKTOP
  2 x 2 IN.
- BATTENS FOR THE
  WALLS 2 x 1 IN.
- 2 x ¹⁄₂-IN. FASCIA
  MOLDING FOR
  THE TOP
- WOOD FILLER
- No. 6 WALL ANCHORS
- 1-IN. PINS
- WOOD GLUE
- SANDPAPER
- PRIMER AND ENAMEL
  OR MATTE PAINT
- SPIRIT LEVEL IN A
  LONG RULE
- PENCIL FOR MARKING
- DRILL WITH A ¹⁄₄-IN.
  MASONRY BIT
- PILOT, CLEARANCE,
  AND COUNTERSINK
  BITS (USE A
  SCREWSINK FOR
  ALL THREE)
- BOX OF 2-IN. No. 6
  SCREWS
- HANDSAW
- SMALL HAMMER
- CENTER PUNCH
- PAINT BRUSH

PROJECT THREE

Making a low worktop

Children's furniture can be expensive to buy, so if you are fitting out a playroom it is well worth building a low, stable work surface. Begin by buying small chairs to match a low work surface, increasing the size of both as the children grow. Think about placing the work surface in a convenient place for electric sockets or wall lights, or in good natural light.

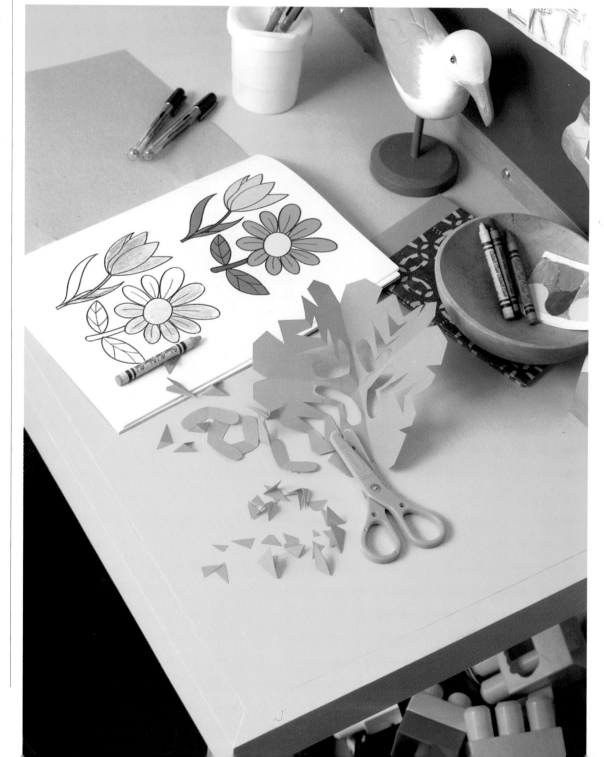

A low work surface is probably the most important item in a children's playroom. It is essential for painting, drawing, coloring-in, and glueing, as well as other learning games.

HOW TO DO IT

STEP 1 Mark the height for the batten on the wall. Cut the batten to the correct length and drill clearance holes every 4 in. Mark these as screw positions on the wall, and then drill and plug the holes.

STEP 2 Screw the batten to the wall. Rest the worktop on the batten and (with help) place the legs in position. Mark their cutting height, having first checked the worktop with the spirit level.

STEP 3 Measure the fascia against the top, and mark the position of the miters.

STEP 4 Glue and pin the fascia boards to the edge of the worktop.

STEP 5 Miter two battens to form a square collar to hold the leg firmly into the corner of the fascia. Screw into position.

STEP 6 Drill clearance holes, and screw through the worktop to secure it to the wall-mounted batten.

- SHEET OF SOFTBOARD (LUMBER MERCHANTS STOCK THIS)
- PANEL ADHESIVE
- "HOCKEY-STICK" MOLDING TO SURROUND THE TOP AND SIDES
- 1½-IN. NO. 6 SCREWS OR 1-IN. BRADS
- WOOD FILLER
- ¼-IN. WALL ANCHORS (IF USING SCREWS TO FIX)
- HANDSAW
- MITER BLOCK
- DRILL WITH NO. 6 MASONRY BIT, OR A SMALL HAMMER AND CENTER PUNCH
- CUPPED BRASS SCREWS

PROJECT FOUR

Fitting a pinboard above the worktop

It is a very good idea to fit a pinboard that runs the length of the worktop. This means that paintings and drawings can be pinned up to dry and be admired. A pinboard can be made from cork tiles or softboard, which is inexpensive; it can be painted any color to match the room.

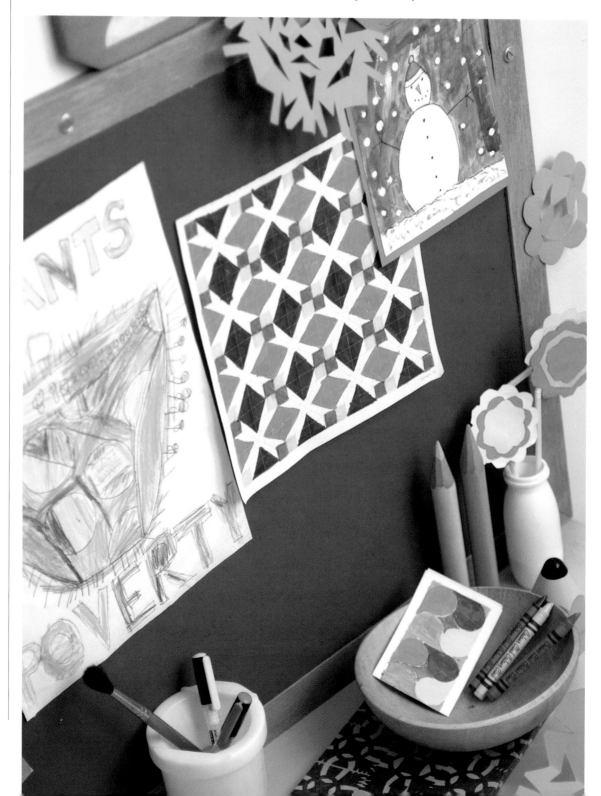

Softboard makes an ideal pinboard because it is lightweight, so it can be stuck to the wall with panel adhesive and painted a favorite color. Some paintings to be proud of will complete the look.

HOW TO DO IT

STEP 1 Measure and cut the softboard to fit. Cut the length of molding for the top edge with mitered ends. Cut the two side pieces mitered to the top but straight at the bottom.

STEP 2 Fix the lower mitered molding on to the wall first, using cupped brass screws.

STEP 3 Fix the rest of the frame to the wall. Apply a long squiggle of panel adhesive to the back of the softboard, and attach to the wall.

Color & light

Selecting colors can be completely daunting—there's such a huge range of choice, it can be difficult to know where to start. But everyone's got their favorites, and it's important to be surrounded by yours. But a combination of color and light can also completely set the mood of a room, so it's useful to know about the qualities of different colors, and the effects they can have. This section describes how colors can be used to create moods and different styles, and how a whole range of different lighting can enhance the function and atmosphere of a room.

Using color to create moods

Color can lift our moods, relax us, stimulate our senses, and even make us feel uncomfortable in certain combinations. According to color theory there are three primary colors—red, yellow, and blue—from which all other colors are derived. To test this, put a blob of each primary color on a white saucer and then mix equal amounts of two colors together. Red and yellow make orange, red and blue make purple, and yellow and blue make green.

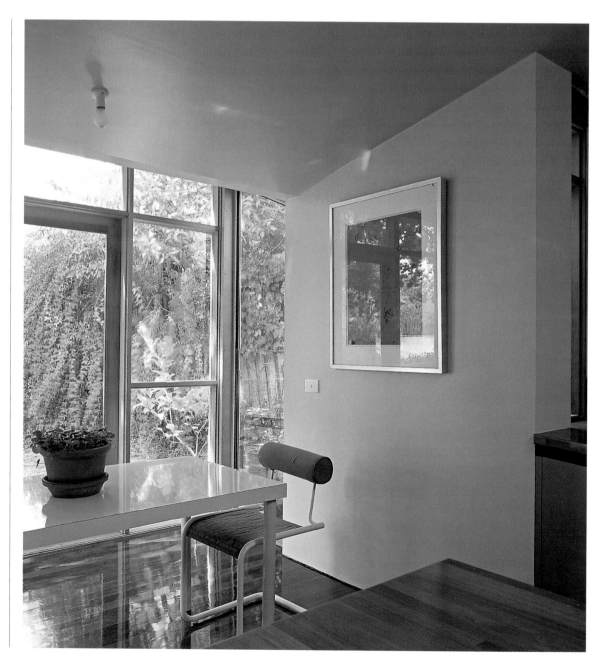

Lilac is a calming color because it is a product of blue, which is said to have a meditative effect. Be careful not to go too dark, though—darker shades of lilac, which become violet purple, can be depressing.

These are the secondary colors, and by adding black or white you can darken or lighten them. By mixing combinations of different amounts of the primaries and black and white you can, in theory, make any imaginable color. It is quite a science, though, and beginners soon discover that most combinations soon turn grey or muddy brown! The paint companies have taken the guesswork out of color mixing for us, and computers are used to dispense just the right amount of each component color so that we can rely on color number 3055b, for instance, to look the same every time.

Choosing colors

When choosing colors for a room, the first consideration should always be to choose a color that you like, regardless of fashion. That is not to say don't experiment, because otherwise you would probably never develop your own ideas. Try to raise your color awareness by noticing combinations of colors that you like. And don't restrict yourself to just looking at color in a decorating context because you may find the best inspiration elsewhere, for instance in a cookery book. A plate of salad, a bowl of fruit, or heaps of vegetables on a market stall could equally provide the key to a brand-new look for one of the rooms in your house. Vacations are also inspirational times, because all our senses are more receptive to pleasure when we are relaxed and away from the pressures of everyday living. Take photographs of the landscape and buildings, the sea, and any unusual color combinations, and then see if you can pick out one color scheme that reminds you of that time and place.

Making a complete color change can be daunting, especially if your inspiration has come from a book or makeover television program

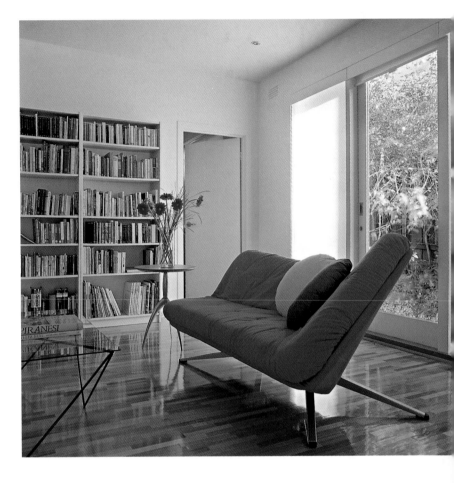

where a room has been professionally styled with co-ordinating furniture and accessories. Strong colors invariably work well on television because the programs need to make an impact in a short time, and there is not much room for subtlety. In your own home conditions are different, and you may find that the ideas that inspired you need to be toned down for everyday life. A strong color is useful for defining the shape of a room and creating an atmosphere. It will set the mood for the whole home when used in the entrance hall, and it is a good way of defining your own space if you are sharing the living space with other people. Blue is a most versatile color and was one of the last to appear in a full range of shades for home decorating because, until recently, the deepest shades were only available as pigments from art suppliers.

Red and yellow fabrics add warmth to a room with a wooden floor and create a modern country look.

This was also noticed with green because it derives from a mixture of blue and yellow. As the range of blues has expanded, so have the greens. The most obvious newcomer that has become tremendously popular is lime green. It is sharp, sassy, and youthful—the color that nobody grew up with! Also note that in hot countries the light is much brighter, and strong colors work better than they do in the pale gray of Northern light. In fact color cannot exist without light, and colored light actually changes painted color.

When darkness falls all color disappears and red, blue, and green become black—it's just a trick of the light!

Warming

If you have a cool room that needs warmth, then use red, yellow, and orange—the effect is immediate and warming. The intrinsic power of a color is not lost in dilution either. A warm yellow could be a rich cream or an earthy ocher. These are the yellows that lean toward red and away from blue. In the same way, choose reds that contain yellow rather than blue, like deep rusty brown, red ocher or deep burnt orange.

To keep a color scheme warm avoid reds, purples, or pinks that contain a lot of blue. These exotic colors, like crimson, violet, and cerise, are good for highlights and flashes of brilliance, but they do not radiate warmth. A rosy pink with pea green and white is a natural combination that is fresh without feeling cool. Choose greens with a deep yellow cast like moss, pea, and olive for warmth. Sage green is a neutral gray-green that can be warmed or cooled by the colors that surround it. Use it with deep reds and mustard yellow for a warm country look. Brown, rust, and deep greens all look good with natural wood and fabrics, and the effect does not have to be old-fashioned or heavy—mix woven fabrics like tweed with leather chairs, wooden flooring, and rugs for a modern country look.

Cooling

In the Northern Hemisphere we tend to choose colors for warmth, but sometimes we need the opposite effect. If the coolness of a room is pleasant and desirable, then enhance the effect with pale greens, icy blue, or pale lemon yellow. Think of the Swedish look, where the whites and grays of the landscape have been brought into

A cool room lacking in natural light can be brightened by white, and this is the perfect background for a crimson spotlight to add a splash of color.

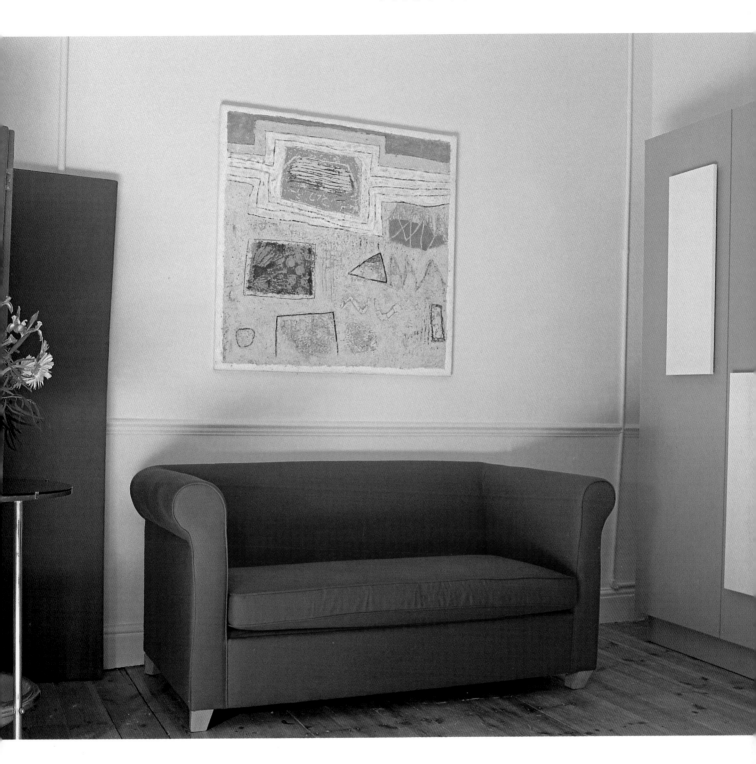

the home. The style is cool and minimal. In the Mediterranean countries houses are painted white to reflect the heat away from the house and keep it cool. Used indoors, white will brighten a cool room that lacks natural light without warming it, and help to create a tranquil atmosphere. All colors look good with white, but the really strong contrasts look best in brilliant sunshine, as in the intense blues and whites of buildings on the Greek islands. A pale sky, or lavender blue and white have an altogether more calming effect.

Red can add warmth to a room. Red and blue together, as two primary colors, make a strong contrast.

The colors of Africa have been brought into this room— the rusty red sofas complement the wooden carvings and floor.

Citrus yellow with gray, black, and white is sharp, cool, and modern, and it looks especially good with the reflective metals like stainless steel, chrome, or aluminum. Black and white are cool but hard, and being the ultimate contrast, are best used where crisp lines are required on tiles, or to make a traditional checkerboard floor.

Creating an atmosphere with color

Certain styles and color schemes are quickly recognizable, for example, New England, African, Caribbean, Far Eastern, and so on. This makes it quite easy for us to recreate a particular atmosphere in our own homes, giving the living room the Moroccan look, or a dining room a

dash of Scandinavian, mostly with the use of color. Different historical periods are also known for their color schemes, which were sometimes more bizarre than you would imagine, and most paint companies produce historically correct colors for use in period homes. This does not mean living in museums and furnishing our homes with all the correct antiques. A Colonial or Victorian room returned to its original colors and furnished in a modern style can look elegant and seriously cool at the same time.

As a rule, light color schemes will provide a lighter atmosphere, and so on. If you want your bedroom to look like a Turkish love nest, begin by getting the color right on the walls—a

(Left) Pinks and purples in these silk and satin cushions suggest an exotic Turkish bazaar.

deep alizarin crimson is as passionate a color as you can get, and has its origins in the Ottoman Empire. Be inspired by color combinations in paintings, carpets, and textiles, and dress up the room with genuine oriental bazaar accessories like metal lanterns, scarves, beadwork, and wall hangings.

Blues and yellows

Deep ultramarine blue is cool and atmospheric, and a room with walls painted this blue will appear bigger. The effect is the opposite to that of deep red, which can make the walls close in! Blue is said to be the perfect meditative color, so choose this for a spiritual atmosphere. Yellow rooms are said to be stimulating to the senses, and for this reason yellow is best avoided in bedrooms, especially of young children, where it might prevent a good night's sleep. Yellow is a good kitchen color, where its positive properties will give you the ideal start to the day. Lavender blue is the opposite—it is very calming, but taken several shades darker to violet purple, it can be depressing, so use purple sparingly unless it is contrasted with an equally powerful color such as lime green, which will neutralize its depressive qualities. These two colors have become such an essential part of the modern decorator's palette that they will probably define our period as clearly as pale green, apricot, and cream did in the early years of the 20th century.

(Above) The warm yellow of these walls is complemented by the Oriental purples of the lampshade, chair cover, and floor cushions.

(Left) Green and white combinations have a fresh, cool effect. If you want a warmer green than the one shown here, choose one with a deep yellow cast, like moss, pea, or olive green.

Using lighting effectively

The first thing to consider when decorating a room is the amount of natural light it gets, and also when it gets the sun. This proportion of natural light and sunlight, and the function of the room will help you make the correct lighting choices. Lighting should never be an afterthought in the decorating process, and is something to consider from the start, especially if new sockets and channels for wall lights are needed. Remember this, and you will never have the depressing task of channeling into a newly plastered and painted wall to fit a wall light!

It is not just color that can affect mood—the way a room is lit can affect the whole atmosphere, so it is worth giving it as much consideration as you do the color, furniture, and accessories. Lighting has to be functional, but it is also aesthetic, so think about the function of the room, as well as the mood you want to set for it. Good illumination can be created by using several different types of lighting, each of which has a different function.

Task lighting

When you are planning the lighting for your room, first decide on which areas need strong light, or task lighting. These should be the work and reading areas, where it is essential for you to be able to see what you are doing. You will also need occasional strong lighting in some areas to illuminate cupboards, bookshelves, hi-fi equipment, or televisions, video recorders, or writing desks.

(Right) Table lamps create pools of low light, which make a room more cozy and intimate.

(Far right) Inspection lamps, spotlights, or just plain flashlights can be used to simulate lighting, so you can buy a type suitable for a particular room.

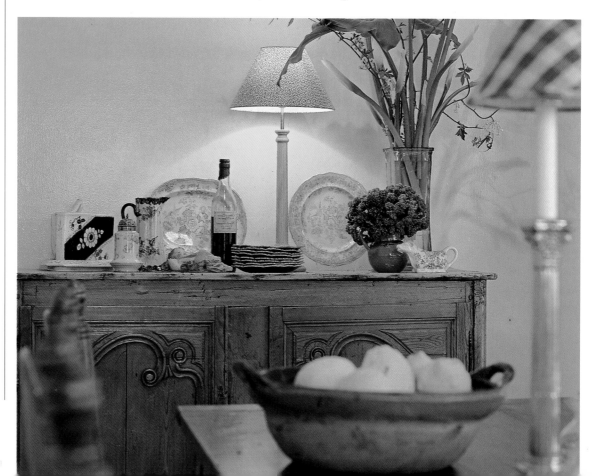

Ambient lighting

Ambient lighting is another way of describing the light that is all around us. This background lighting simulates the natural daylight and takes the glare out of direct task lighting. Ambient light reveals the shape and size of the room, and the colors used in it. A pendant fitting or a wall light fits this description.

Accent lighting

This type of lighting is either purely decorative, where the light itself is the decorative feature, or it is used to highlight and accentuate a piece of furniture or art in the room.

Buying lighting

Lighting is not an easy thing to buy because, unlike other products, where you look before you buy, if you go to a crowded lighting showroom with no idea of what you are looking for, it will be practically impossible to judge the effect of an individual light when so many others are turned on. The best idea is to decide what kind of light you need and experiment in your home before you go out and buy it. Look in lighting catalogs for the different kinds of lights available, and magazines for how they look in situ. Then experiment by using flashlights, plug-in spotlights, and inspection lamps to simulate wall washers, uplighters, downlighters, pendant lights, spotlights, and table lamps. This is a job for two or more people, so invite friends round with their flashlights and turn a task into a party! There are lots of good lighting catalogs that supply goods by mail order, so there is no reason to feel limited to what is available locally. Most suppliers also understand the importance of seeing a lamp in your own room, and will be happy to exchange or refund when you return a light for purely esthetic reasons.

Creating illusions

If you use a room during the day and it gets very little sunlight, you can make a room seem much sunnier by concealing white fluorescent tubes beneath valances above the windows. Daytime lighting is often necessary, especially in winter, but bulbs tend to create an unpleasant glare in natural daylight. Fit concealed halogen spotlights behind plants or furniture, and fluorescent striplights beneath wall cupboards to light worktops. Make any room appear more spacious by washing the walls with light from above or below. Disguise any features you dislike in a room by using angled spotlights to cast pools of light in another direction. A pendant light will appear to lower the ceiling height to where the light begins; use pendants in small rooms with high ceilings to change the proportions. A room will look more cosy and intimate with table lamps creating pools of low light.

Colored lights

Tinted bulbs are useful for creating an atmosphere. Pale yellow will warm the room, and pink will create a rosy glow. Stronger-colored bulbs will knock out some of the colors completely—red or green cancel each other out, and blue will give a cool nightclub effect that is perfect for summer parties. Red has the opposite effect, making a cool room seem instantly warmer. Christmas lights are also useful for adding instant sparkle, and use very little electricity. Put them around pictures, doorways, or in glass fishbowls as feature lights with a party feel.

Candles

Candles give a room a unique atmosphere, and there has never been more choice than there is today. Gone are the days when a scented candle smelled like an air freshener—one candle can cost

as much as a table lamp, but the scents on offer are so sublime that stores have trouble keeping up with the demand. The flicker of candlelight is the most romantic and relaxing type of light, and rows of nightlights bring a room to life.

Safety

There is one big downside to the candle boom, and that is the rise in the number of house fires. Always use common sense when you site your candles, and never place them where there is the slightest chance of flames catching paper or fabric. It is also important not to leave candles burning unattended, but because while we all love to walk into a candlelit room, we can also ignore the safety advice. Very real danger comes from falling asleep, or actually leaving the house with a candle burning: this should *never* be done.

Uplighters can make a ceiling look higher by casting it with light from below.

(Far left) Halogen spotlights cast an ambient light that can be angled to cast pools in different directions.

Accessories

The finishing touches you add to a room are a chance to put a little of yourself into the style, whether it be in an arrangement of pictures, a choice of mirrors, a pile of cushions, or a display of flowers. These final choices are fun to make, and usually take the least amount of time and effort. But they can also make or break the whole effect. This section gives a few things to think about when you're choosing these final touches.

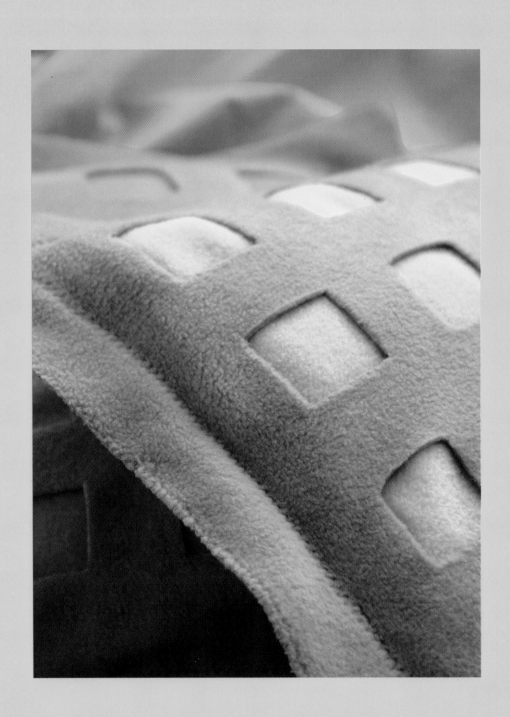

Accessories

The dictionary defines an accessory as "a thing that is extra, useful, or decorative, but not essential." These are the finishing touches to have some fun with when the paint has dried, the flooring is down, and the curtains are up. This is where we allow our individuality to shine through, making our rooms reflect our lifestyles and personalities.

Walls without pictures or mirrors can make a room seem cold and unfriendly. Pictures are an ideal way of adding a splash of individuality to your walls.

Magazines and mail-order catalogs all use stylists, who are to rooms what hair and make-up people are to celebrities. The stylist's job involves keeping track of everything that already exists and is new to the accessory market, and their real skill is in knowing how to accessorize to best effect. Thanks to these tireless hunter-gatherers, we get tons of visual reference and no shortage of shopping information. Treat yourself to a selection of different sources of inspiration—a good weekend color supplement, a monthly homes magazine, or a range of mail-order catalogs.

A room with individuality will often include a mixture of old and new objects, or at least things sourced from different places: a set of matching cushions from a chain store, for instance, used next to an unusual lamp from a specialist lighting store. Similar objects in varying styles will create areas of interest that will catch the eye. Black and white photographs arranged in a block of four matching frames on the wall will look smart and stylish, but a bit cold and contrived. Add one brightly colored picture in an intricately carved wooden frame on a tabletop, and the atmosphere will change immediately.

Not everything needs to be unique or expensive, and it is worth perusing a few of the style magazines' "best-buy" pages for recommendations. Keep a look out for the price comparison features, which show very similar designs with massive price differentials. You may fall in love with an impossibly expensive wrought-iron candelabra, and be lucky enough to discover an almost identical version in a cheaper hardware outlet. Decorating has become very much like fashion and clothing in this way, with new styles sourced at the top end of the market then copied and quickly reproduced for mass consumption. Great news for the consumer, not so good for the designers under constant pressure to change styles and create new looks.

Frames and pictures

Walls without pictures or mirrors seem to absorb energy and interest from the room and, depending on their color, can also make a room seem cold and unfriendly. There are so many framing options that it can be very confusing, and the right frame can make an ordinary image look impressive or quite the opposite. As a simple rule, most things look best with some white space around them, and a small image needs the most space between it and the frame. Sets of matching frames can look brilliant with very simple images of fruit or flowers, bold, colorful art postcards, or something more graphic, like letters of the alphabet or stamped numbers. The frames themselves can be the stars, especially if you trawl through antique and bric-à-brac markets. An ornate molding can look fabulous around the most unlikely image. If you lack confidence, then buy framed prints from a good furniture and accessory store, or a small gallery. The actual act of looking for something to put on your walls will soon make you aware of what appeals to you and what doesn't. Ideally, you should find something that will give you pleasure every time you look at it.

Cushions and throws

Gone are the days when a change of upholstery cost a small fortune—now all that's needed on an elderly sofa or chair is a new throw and a couple of cushions. Throws do a lot more than just disguising marks on the upholstery, though, they are also useful for introducing a strong color contrast, a more casual, relaxed style, and a real sense of comfort. A throw can be the same color as the sofa but a very different texture, for instance, mohair on linen, or velvet on leather. Cushions and throws can be co-ordinated in fabric, texture, or color, but beware of too many matching accessories—they can make a home look like a hotel. If you are short of money but want a new look, buy a large cotton decorator's dustsheet and a packet of machine dye to make a giant throw to cover an old sofa. Spend any money left over on lovely cushions, or buy cushion pads and make the covers yourself. For color and sparkle

at a reasonable price buy Indian or Chinese fabric; for florals, buy an old chintz curtain and add a nice trimming; for knitted woolens or plain cottons, adapt old shirts and sweaters by cutting off the arms and sewing up the top and bottom seams— the buttons stay put.

Vases, flowers and plants

If you allow yourself just one treat for the house once a week, make it a vase of fresh flowers. Even a bunch of wild flowers in a bottle on a wooden fruit box will make a house look like a home. Vases can be square, round, tall, or short, and be made of glass or ceramic. They can even be left empty and still look good on a shelf. This is a way to add accent color that can be changed to suit your mood. If fresh flowers don't match your busy lifestyle, then get a plant or two. Very beautiful house plants are often low-maintenance in the right position, which is usually near light and out of drafts. Larger, more architectural plants, like palm, bamboo, cacti, and the good old money plant, look good in contemporary surroundings. If you prefer something smaller with flowers, then orchids are the current must-haves.

Throws are an effective way of introducing a strong color contrast, a more relaxed style, and a sense of comfort.

Mini projects

Starting big decorating projects can be daunting, so it's best to begin by tackling something small and satisfying, so you can get your creative steam up and find that one thing leads to another. These projects will not take very long to complete and don't cost very much, but have been designed to give maximum satisfaction with minimum effort. A room can be perked up with new cushions, frames, and lampshades, and sometimes all that is needed is a makeover for your existing accessories.

MINI PROJECT ONE
Lampshades

YOU WILL NEED:
- A SELECTION OF
  BUTTONS
- TUBE OF CLEAR GLUE
- LAMPSHADE

It is often difficult to find a lampshade to match the color scheme of your room, but there is no need to worry because lampshades can be painted with ordinary latex paint, and a test pot of color will be enough to transform two medium-sized shades or one large one. Plain colors look great, but patterns can be stamped or stenciled on, and you can also add trimmings such as a fringe, baubles, or beads in contrasting or harmonizing colors. The lampshade in the project is embellished with buttons stuck on with clear glue. Before the throwaway culture took over, every home had a button tin, and nowadays these often turn up at flea markets and thrift shops. Old buttons can be really beautiful, and even the plain shell or mother-of-pearl types are well worth showing off on a lampshade or cushion cover.

Bases of lamps can be decorated as well as the shades. This seaside-style lamp base has been given a wet sand effect with shells attached using strong glue.

HOW TO DO IT

STEP 1 Plan the arrangement of the buttons on the shade. Apply a blob of glue to each.

STEP 2 Hold it firmly against the shade until you feel the glue bonding. Continue with this until you have used all your chosen buttons.

YOU WILL NEED:
- 19½ IN. FLEECE FABRIC IN COLOR A
- 19½ IN. OF COLOR B FABRIC HALF THE WIDTH OF COLOR A
- RULE
- CRAFT KNIFE
- SEWING MACHINE
- SCISSORS
- THREAD
- PINS
- CARDBOARD TEMPLATE FOR CUT-OUT
- PEN

MINI PROJECT TWO

Cushions

There is no need to put up with grubby or faded cushions, when a new set of covers is all you need to inject a bit of fresh style into the room. If your cushions feel lumpy, be bold and throw them away, then treat yourself to some new ones. Cushion pads are not expensive, and fabric can be bought either in remnant lengths or by the foot. Check out thrift stores and markets for lengths of fabric or clothing that can be cut down to make cushion covers. Shirts and cardigans make great covers, as they already have a buttoned opening, and you simply have to sew across under the arms and then cut off the top and the bottom. Evening dresses can be transformed into wonderfully exotic cushion covers for the boudoir, and an odd velvet curtain could be used to make a whole new set of cushions. There is also a lot of fun to be had with dyes and trimmings. If the bug really bites you, you could end up selling designer cushions from a stall of your own!

This stylish cushion cover can be made from fleece or felt, neither of which fray when cut, so they will need no hemming. Fleece has the advantage of being washable, so is the best choice if you want the cushions to last a while, and if you use a washable pad, then the cushion can go in the washing machine and tumble drier.

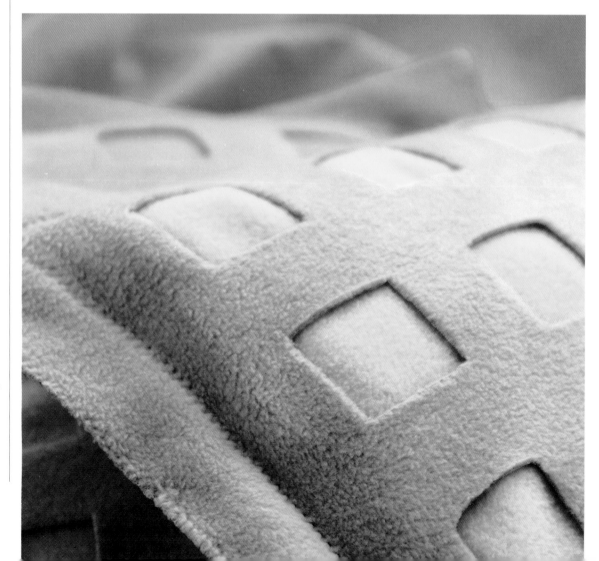

A two-colored cushion cover made out of fleece fabric is easy to make, and if used with a washable cushion pad, it can be put in the washing machine and drier.

HOW TO DO IT

STEP 1 Cut out three squares of fabric in the same size—two in color A and one in color B.

STEP 2 Mark the cut-outs by drawing around the template on the back of the color B square. Use the craft knife and straight edge to cut out the shapes.

STEP 3 Place the color B square on top of the other two and sew a line of close zigzag stitches to join the three layers on three sides. Put the cushion pad inside, then sew up the fourth side.

Frames

YOU WILL NEED:
• FOIL WRAPPERS FROM
  CANDY AND
  CHOCOLATES
• PVA GLUE
• SIMPLE FRAME
• SCISSORS OR A
  SNAP-BLADE KNIFE

Framed pictures on the walls make a house look like home, and there is no need to have bare walls just because you think you don't have any art worth framing. Make the frames into a focal point, and put anything inside them that fits in with the shape and color scheme. You will be surprised how effective this can look. If your frame is square, then pay a visit to a card store and check out all the square cards. Once everyday objects are framed they assume a new importance, and can even become art! Try framing groups of bottle caps, buttons, labels, or some unusual foreign packaging—most of these things have been designed by experts, so why not put them on show? When it comes to the actual frames, these can be picked up secondhand for next to nothing at yard sales or from market stalls. New frames from bargain stores can also be used, and sometimes all that is needed is a coat of paint to give them a new lease of life. Buy matching sets and paint them different colors, or buy lots of different frames and make them into a set by painting them a matching color. There are so many ways in which they can be improved— it's just up to you to do it.

This wooden frame was about as plain and cheap as anything new can be, but now looks a million dollars with its shiny, jewel-colored covering. The metallic papers are candy wrappers (yes, you have to eat the candy first!), which are carefully smoothed out and stuck onto the frame in a patchwork pattern using PVA glue. This project is pure pleasure, from start to finish.

Old picture frames or cheap, new ones can be given this sparkling, jewel effect using candy wrappers and glue. Try framing everyday objects inside to create an original work of art!

HOW TO DO IT

STEP 1 Smooth out enough candy wrappers to cover the frame. They will need to overlap each other, and look best in a random patchwork pattern. Lay them out to decide on the color arrangement.

STEP 2 Apply a coat of PVA to the frame, and then leave it to become tacky. Apply a coat of PVA to the back of each wrapper.

STEP 3 Smooth each wrapper onto the frame. Take care not to rip the fragile foil as you flatten it around the shape of the frame.

STEP 4 Use a sponge to ease the foil papers onto the frame, and then wipe away any excess glue.

Index

Notes

Notes

Acknowledgments

The authors would particularly like to thank Clare Shanahan,
for her irrepressible good humor, patience, and expert
styling of the photographs.
They would also like to thank Alistair's mum Doris
for her patience during the photoshoot.

The publishers would like to thank the following UK companies for loan of props:
Embrotrap (Oriental) Market, 10 Church Road, Hove, East Sussex;
Evolution, 42 Bond Street, Brighton, East Sussex;
Interior Illusions, 46 High Street, Old Town, Hastings;
Middle Farm, Firle, East Sussex;
Saffron, 21 Bond Street, Brighton, East Sussex;
The Ship Wreck Center, Rock-an-Ore, Hastings, East Sussex;
Stewart Gallery, 48 Devonshire Road, Bexhill, East Sussex;
Sussex Marble, 16 Wainwright Close, St. Leonards on Sea, East Sussex;
T.C. Carpets and Beds, Earl Street, Hastings, East Sussex;
W.H.Clarke Scaffolding, Hackney Road, London;
Wood Bros, 66 George Street, Brighton, East Sussex.

The publishers would also like to thank the following for use of copyright material:
ELIZABETH WHITING & ASSOCIATES: pp. 10, 11, 18, 19, 26, 27, 34, 35, 44, 45, 46, 54, 55, 56, 57, 62, 63, 71, 78, 79,
86, 87, 92, 93, 100, 101, 108, 109, 110, 111, 116, 117, 122, 123, 132, 133, 140, 141, 146, 147, 156, 157, 158, 159, 168, 169,
176, 177, 186, 187, 192, 193, 194, 195, 202, 203, 212, 213, 214, 215, 226, 227, 228, 229, 230, 231, 232, 233, 234, 235, 238, 239, 242.